THE LITTLE BOOK OF
ARSENAL

AN ARSENAL A to Z

Written by Ian Welch and Michael Heatley

THE LITTLE BOOK OF
ARSENAL

This edition first published in the UK in 2007
By Green Umbrella Publishing

www.gupublishing.co.uk

Publishers Jules Gammond & Vanessa Gardner

Printed and Bound by Butler and Tanner

ISBN-13: 978-1-905009-86-2

football to lengthen his Arsenal career. His last game for England was in October 2000, when Germany beat England 0-1.

Back with his club, Adams skippered the Gunners to their unique 1993 FA Cup and Coca-Cola Cup double against Sheffield Wednesday, and when he lifted the European Cup Winners' Cup in Copenhagen the following year, became the man to hoist more trophies than any previous Arsenal captain. Indeed, he captained Arsenal to League titles in three different decades, a unique achievement.

True to his quote 'Arsenal is a great club and a successful one, so why should I want to play for anyone else?' Adams retired from playing professional football in 2002. A spell as manager of Wycombe Wanderers proved unsuccessful, but he split his time between studying the game and running the Sporting Chance clinic for sportsmen who, like him, had struggled with addiction to drink or drugs. (His autobiography, *Addicted*, was published in 1999.)

ABOVE Adams slides in to tackle Steve Bushell of Blackpool during the 1999 FA Cup Third Round match played at Highbury winning 3-1

Allison

GEORGE ALLISON, BORN IN DARLIngton in 1885, was a journalist who commentated on the radio during Arsenal's Cup Final defeat to Cardiff City in 1927. He joined the club and served as secretary and managing director before taking over from Herbert Chapman as manager after the latter's sudden death through pneumonia in 1934. He was in charge as they completed an historic trio of top-flight titles in 1935, adding another Championship in 1938 to an FA Cup win in 1936. His team attracted Arsenal's all-time record Highbury crowd, 73,295, who turned up to see the game against Sunderland in March 1935.

Sadly the advent of World War II interrupted Allison's managerial career, though he was credited as technical advisor in the film *The Arsenal Stadium Mystery* (1940) and made a cameo role as himself uttering the immortal words 'One-nil to the Arsenal'. (He is credited as Arsenal manager from 1934-47, but six years were effectively lost.)

After a transitional Gunners side lacking many of its pre-war stars came 13th in the first peacetime season, Allison stepped down from the job in favour of Tom Whittaker. He died in 1957.

BELOW George Allison, Arsenal manager

Armstrong

'HE WAS THE ORIGINAL MANAGER'S dream… he could play on the right or left, had excellent technical ability and the biggest heart.' That was Bertie Mee's assessment of 'Geordie' Armstrong, the wiry winger who was a mainstay of the Double-winning side of 1970-71.

Armstrong was voted Player of the Year in 1970 and, having completed his apprenticeship as an electrician before entering football, was very much one of the people. It's surprising the Durham dynamo (born in Hebburn on 9 August 1944) who'd had trials with Grimsby and Newcastle before joining Arsenal as an amateur didn't improve on his five England Under-23 caps that followed youth honours. But then he was vying with Alan Ball, the man who'd ironically join him in the Highbury engine-room from 1971-76. His strike rate was unimpressive – 53 in exactly 500 League appearances giving an almost exact one-in-ten ratio – but his worth to the side was immense.

After making his final first-team appearance on a summer 1977 tour of Australia, Armstrong played just two seasons away from Highbury at Leicester (after a £15,000 transfer that September) and Stockport. But his heart never left and he returned to become reserve-team coach after spells on the staff of Aston Villa, Fulham, Middlesbrough and posts in Kuwait and Norway. George Armstrong died in November 2000.

ABOVE Armstrong demonstrates some fancy footwork, 1971

Ashburton Grove

AFTER NEARLY A CENTURY AT Highbury, Arsenal decided in 1999 to develop a new stadium at nearby Ashburton Grove. Annual match day revenue of £28 million was dwarfed by TV income of £52 million, mostly generated by participation in the Champions League, which of course could not be guaranteed. The increase in capacity to 60,000 would see the new stadium support nearly 50 per cent of the club's income, increasing matchday earnings by about £20m a season and reducing reliance on Champions League and broadcasting revenues.

Contents

Adams

TONY ADAMS (BORN 10 October 1966) made his League debut in November 1983, the month after he turned 17, given his first chance by another great central defender, then-manager Terry Neill. All went well, but two years later his hopes of becoming David O'Leary's partner were halted by a stress fracture of the right foot. Martin Keown moved in but moved on to Villa after a contract dispute, and Tony made the most of his second chance. His place was never threatened after that, and Arsenal's Player of the Year award came in 1987, confirming that Tony Adams had arrived.

England boss Bobby Robson made it Tony's year, selecting him for the full team and remarking that he had 'such great stature for someone so young.' He went on to play a part in the European Championships, scoring against Yugoslavia in the qualifiers and against the USSR in the 1990 Finals. In between times, he'd played a part in securing the 1987 Littlewoods Cup and, of course, captained the side that took the Championship twice – in spellbinding style at Anfield in 1989, and two years later in 1990-91. He was the lynchpin of a steadfast Arsenal defence under George Graham that was renowned for its well organised use of the offside trap.

Adams was not to wear an England shirt that season, but Graham Taylor recalled him to play in all the 1992-93 World Cup qualifiers, and he remained in favour with Terry Venables. After 66 appearances (13 times as skipper) and 5 goals, he decided to quit international

The move was originally scheduled for August 2005, but this was postponed a year as funding for the stadium project proved problematic. But construction work finally began at the new stadium site in early 2004. The stadium was built by the company responsible for the Stade De France in Paris and boasted a similar roof design along with four tiered stands.

Naming rights were granted to the Emirates airline, but the project's financial impact was still a concern to fans. Arsenal claimed the multi million pound loan taken out to fund the stadium would be spread over 25 years and would not impinge on the playing budget. Arsenal's players reverted to the 'redcurrant' kit worn for the first season at Highbury (1913-14) to celebrate their last match before relocation 600 metres up the road.

ABOVE Inside the Emirates Stadium during the UEFA Champions League match against PSV Eindhoven

Attendances

RECORDS WERE SET THROUGHOUT the Emirates Stadium's first season, 2006-07, an average of around 59,640 comparing favourably with the 38,000 that Highbury had accommodated in recent seasons. For instance, 60,132 witnessed a

2-1 victory over Reading in March 2007. A massive crowd of 73,295 watched a 0-0 draw with Sunderland on 9 March 1935 during George Allison's side's League Championship-winning season.

The club's highest attendance for a 'home' game, however, was registered not at Highbury, but at Wembley. The club played their UEFA Champions' League matches there during the 1998-99 and 1999-2000 seasons and 73,707 people watched RC Lens win 1-0 on 25 November 1998.

The biggest attendance at Highbury since the inauguration of the Premiership was on 15 May 2004 when 38,419 fans crammed into the stadium to watch Patrick Vieira lift the Premiership trophy after a 2-1 win over Leicester City completed Arsenal's famous unbeaten season.

Although the lowest recorded figure of 4,554 for the visit of Leeds United on 5 May 1966 is paltry compared to today's attendances, Arsenal's lowest Premiership crowd is still respectable by some top-flight team's standards. Only 18,253 paid to watch the visit of Wimbledon on 10 February 1993 and the majority would have been disappointed as the visitors claimed the points with a solitary Dean Holdsworth goal.

Ball

BORN ON 12 MAY 1945 IN Farnworth, Lancashire, Alan Ball was the son of a professional footballer/manager, also Alan, but eclipsed his dad in every respect by becoming a World Cup winner with England in 1966. He then moved on to Everton, from where an Arsenal record fee of £220,000 tempted him to Highbury at the end of 1971.

The fiery midfielder with a temper to match his red hair was intended to help Bertie Mee's team retain the title – this did not happen, but Ball was at the peak of his powers at 26 and became the captain of Don Revie's England team. His 72 appearances in white yielded eight goals. His Arsenal career of 177 appearances and 45 goals sadly coincided with a period of mediocrity

and, while an influential figure on the pitch, he was not to win domestic honours in red and white.

After joining Southampton in 1976 and helping them to the top flight, Ball spent time in the North American Soccer League before returning home to start a managerial career with the likes of Portsmouth (twice) and Manchester City. Alan Ball died in April 2007, aged just 61, and was much mourned.

ABOVE Alan Ball of Arsenal in action against Manchester City at Highbury

Bastin

BELOW The youngest player on the books at Arsenal, Cliff Bastin, 1930

BORN IN EXETER ON 14 MARCH 1912, Cliff Bastin's arrival at Highbury in 1929 as a teenage winger from local club

BELOW The youngest player on the books at Arsenal, Cliff Bastin, 1930

Exeter City coincided with Herbert Chapman perfecting his footballing formula. Bastin, a bargain at just £2,000, would leave Arsenal's employ with five League Championships plus two FA Cup winner's medals. Indeed, he was the only member of the triumphant side that carried all before it in the pre-war decade to see first-team action in 1946-47, the first peacetime season.

He topped the club's scoring chart in 1932-33 with 33 goals, a prodigious haul for a winger, and would remain the club's overall top scorer until 1997 when his goals total was beaten by Ian Wright (and since, of course, by Thierry Henry). He played for England 21 times, scoring 12 goals, and would undoubtedly have registered many more honours for club and country had Hitler not intervened.

Forever known as 'Boy' in deference to his youth, Cliff Bastin died in December 1991, his first club Exeter City naming a stand in his honour.

Bergkamp

DENNIS BERGKAMP, BORN IN Amsterdam on 10 May 1969, was named after Denis Law (despite the spelling) by his soccer-mad father. Arsenal rescued him in 1995 from two miserable years with Inter Milan, where he was in and out of the team, often as substitute, and he paid back the club record £7.5 million fee with interest over the decade that followed.

Bergkamp made his name in the great Ajax Amsterdam team that ruled European club football. There he enjoyed a memorable strike partnership with Stefan Petterson, and he was quick to link with Ian Wright at Arsenal. Both helped each other to improve their game, and the Dutchman gave Arsenal an extra dimension.

At Highbury, he wore the Number 10 shirt from the 1995-96 season kick-off, mocking the critics who claimed he would follow his Milan nightmare with another in London. He supplanted the London rivals Spurs' just-departed Jürgen Klinsmann as the highest-profile import in the Premiership.

Indeed, Bergkamp dominated the division in 1997-98, leading Arsenal to the title. He was forced to miss the Cup Final through injury but was voted 'Player of the Year' by his PFA peers and came third in the voting for 'FIFA Player of the Year'. Arsène Wenger, who inherited him from Bruce Rioch, con-

ABOVE Bergkamp celebrates scoring the opening goal during the Champions League match against Borussia Dortmund at Highbury in 2002

sidered him 'at the peak of his career – I don't think there's anybody better in the world.'

He shone in the World Cup in France '98 but a subsequent back injury put him out of the first half of the next campaign and he bowed out of international football after Euro 2000. His record was 79 games played, 37 goals scored.

The second Double season of 2001-02 saw him play a major role. A pair of wonder goals against Leverkusen in the Champions League and a few days later against Newcastle made headlines. After the Double was achieved he admitted 'I've never, ever been this happy in my entire career.' He passed the 100th goal mark in January 2003 and the following season (2004-05) helped steer the side to another title triumph, sometimes wearing the captain's armband.

Surrounded by controversy at various times in his Highbury career – not least because of the fear of flying that ruled him out of many crucial European away matches – his full appearances have diminished as time goes on. His north London stay ended in 2006, but Bergkamp can be assured he is one of the greats.

Brady

TO SAY THAT LIAM BRADY (BORN IN Dublin on 13 February 1956) could play a bit is rather like saying that Arsène Wenger is a reasonable manager. Elegant, comfortable on the ball and a supremely intelligent creative midfielder, Brady became an Arsenal hero virtually as soon as he left the bench, aged 17, to replace Jeff Blockley against Birmingham in October 1973. It was the first of more than 300 appearances for the club.

Brady was born in Dublin on 13 February 1956. He joined Arsenal as a 15-year-old apprentice in June 1971. Brady had a useful right foot – but his left foot was sublime. However, the slight-of-frame Brady was no midfield poser; he was a grafting team player whose skill matched his industry. And he was a player always liable to pop up with a spectacular goal.

By 1974 Brady was a first-team regular and had acquired the nickname 'Chippy', not for his uncanny abilities with the ball but because of his love of chips! He was unfortunate in that Arsenal had lost their way since their remarkable Double season, 1970-71, and while at Highbury he picked up just one winner's medal –

ABOVE Brady on the ball during a Division One match, 1979

LEFT Bergkamp waves as he leads his son Mitchell onto the pitch to say goodbye to his fans after his testimonial match at the Emirates Stadium

and only then because of his man-of-the-match performance as Manchester United were eventually pipped 3-2 at Wembley in 1979.

With four minutes remaining Arsenal were cruising to a routine 2-0 win – Chippy having set up both, for Brian Talbot and Frank Stapleton – only for

RIGHT Liam Brady competes for the Charity Shield against Liverpool, 1979

BELOW Brady during the European Cup Winners' Cup Final, 1980

United to bring the scores level. With extra-time looming, Brady carried the ball down the left wing and crossed for Alan Sunderland to net a dramatic last-gasp winner. In 1978 and 1980 Arsenal had to make do with being FA Cup runners-up, and Brady was culpable in the 1980 Cup Winners' Cup Final as, along with Graham Rix, he missed a penalty in the 1980 Cup Winners' Cup final shootout won by Valencia.

More palatable was the 5-0 destruction of Spurs at White Hart Lane in December 1978 when Brady turned on a midfield masterclass and scored the goal of the season. Arsenal Player of the Year three times, PFA Player of the Year in 1979, and capped 72 times in all for the Republic of Ireland, Brady broke many an Arsenal fans heart when he decided to move on; most, however, realised he needed a greater challenge.

In summer 1980 Brady joined Italian giants Juventus and in two seasons picked up two Serie A Championship medals. He remained in Italy, moving to Sampdoria, Inter Milan and Ascoli before returning to London to play for West Ham. Following his retirement in 1990, he managed Celtic and Brighton before returning to Arsenal as head of youth development and Academy director.

Buchan

BORN IN LONDON ON 22 September 1891, Charlie Buchan slipped through Arsenal's fingers as an amateur when he was allowed to join Clapton Orient and returned to Highbury from Sunderland where he had become the club's all-time leading goalscorer and blossomed to captain his country. Because of the war he only won six England caps but scored four goals.

His transfer fee was a straight £2,000 plus £100 per goal, of which there were 21 in his first season. Though 34 years old when transferred, he was very influential in Herbert Chapman's first Arsenal team. He is credited with devising the WM formation, with the stopper centre-half, that would bring such success, and he shared his tactical acumen with the world when he commentated for the BBC and wrote for the *News Chronicle* newspaper – the first player turned pundit – after retiring in 1928.

Though his only honour at Arsenal was an FA Cup runners-up medal, from the 1927 Final when Cardiff won by a freak goal, Buchan was one of Arsenal's most influential players of the inter-war era. He died in June 1960

ABOVE Arsenal and England footballer, Charles Buchan, 1925

Campbell

RIGHT Captain Campbell celebrates his second goal against Everton at Highbury, 2005

BELOW Campbell during the Premiership match against Manchester City, 2006

AN IMPOSING CENTRAL defender for both Arsenal and England, 31-year-old Sulzeer 'Sol' Campbell (born 18 September 1974) has always been a favourite of the Highbury faithful despite travelling across North London from rivals Tottenham Hotspur in the summer of 2001. The highly acrimonious transfer was proof, as if it were needed, that Campbell had reached the top of his game – having cemented his place as half of England's central defensive duo along with Tony Adams, who he would later play with in his first season with the Gunners. Arsène Wenger was obviously attracted to Campbell's strong and powerful approach to the game – not to mention surprising pace and an eye for a good header, particularly at set pieces.

A surprise addition to England's Euro '96 squad, Sol really made his name at the World Cup two years later with his solid performances, and his affinity with the fans grew after his would-be match-winning header against Argentina was ruled out after a foul in the box. The most senior player of England's central defensive trio along with John Terry and Rio Ferdinand, Campbell's international experience is unsurpassed, and he was the first England international to appear in five successive major tournaments when he played in the 2004 European championships.

Citing participation in the Champions League as one of the main reasons for leaving Spurs, Campbell's decision to join the Gunners was fully justified when they won the FA Cup and Premiership in his first season. Arsenal went on to regain the Premiership crown two years later, a culmination of the now-famous unbeaten season in which Campbell played a big part with 35 first-team appearances. Despite his defensive position, Campbell has the ability to conduct business at the other end of the pitch, his career total well into double digits.

Campbell's leadership qualities have also never been in doubt. He was given the England captaincy almost two years to the day after he was handed his debut, was Spurs club captain and has skippered Arsenal on numerous occasions, smoothing the transition of Patrick Vieira leaving the club in the summer of 2005. Campbell followed Vieira out of the club after a disappointing 2005-06 season, surprisingly ending up on the south coast at Portsmouth.

ABOVE Sol Campbell heads the ball away from Walter Pandiani during their Premiership match at home to Birmingham, October 2005

Champions League

ARSENAL'S 2005-06 SEASON CLImaxed in Paris in May with the Champions League Final against Barcelona. Sadly, the referee did not read the script, and the needless dismissal of Jens Lehmann saw the 10-man Gunners finally overhauled after taking the lead.

The club's first two forays in the premier European competition saw them fail to progress from the group stage having been pitted against RC Lens, Panathinaikos and Dynamo Kiev in 1998-99 and Barcelona, Fiorentina and AIK Solna the following season.

They reached the quarter-finals in 2000-01 having seen off Sparta Prague, Shakhtar Donetsk and Lazio with four wins and a draw in the first group stage before being drawn with Spartak Moscow, Bayern Munich and Lyon in the second. Goals from Parlour and Henry sealed a 2-1 home advantage but a 1-0 away defeat saw Valencia through to the next round on the away goals rule.

The first group stage of the 2001-02 competition saw the Gunners win their three home matches against Mallorca, Schalke and Panathinaikos but fail to collect a single point on their travels. Second-phase victories at home over Juventus (3-1) and Bayer Leverkusen (4-1) were not enough to book their passage to the next round, having lost both matches against Deportivo.

The following season saw a similar fate as Arsenal registered wins over Borussia Dortmund, PSV Eindhoven and Auxerre in the first group stage but could only manage a solitary victory away to Roma in the second. Four draws

followed before a 2-1 defeat in Valencia ended their hopes.

The competition was reorganised in 2003-04 and now consisted of just one group stage followed by knockout rounds. Safe passage was steered past Inter Milan, Lokomotiv Moscow and Dynamo Kiev in the group stage and Celta Vigo in the first knockout fixture. Chelsea were the quarter-final opponents but, having secured a 1-1 draw at Stamford Bridge, Arsenal went down 2-1 in the home leg.

Arsenal emerged undefeated from the 2004-05 group stage with PSV Eindhoven, Rosenborg and Panathinaikos but were unable to recover from the 3-1 defeat away to Bayern Munich in the next round.

Five victories (FC Thun twice, Sparta Prague twice and away to Ajax) and one draw (Ajax at home) in the group stage of 2005-06 saw Arsenal paired with Real Madrid in the first knockout round. Henry's strike in Madrid proved to be the only goal of the tie and the Gunners went on to face Juventus in the quarter-finals. A penalty save by Jens Lehmann in the last minute of the semi-final second leg against Villareal saw them safely through to the Final. The score? One-nil to the Arsenal!

Chapman

BORN IN SHEFFIELD ON 19 January 1878, Herbert Chapman ironically made his name as a player with local rivals Spurs before starting a managerial career that would see him become Arsenal's most successful pre-Wenger boss. His first post as player-manager of Northampton saw them Southern League Champions, and despite suspension when next club Leeds City were investigated for irregularities, he led Huddersfield to the FA Cup and two consecutive League Championships. They made it three in 1926, but by then he was at Arsenal.

Chapman's reign saw many changes made, notably in tactics designed to exploit the new offside law by pulling the centre-half out of midfield and making him the 'last man' (a tactic that became synonymous with the club). Alex James, Eddie Hapgood, David Jack and Cliff Bastin were among the recruits that made his team creatively as well as defensively successful.

FA Cup success came in 1930 with a win against Huddersfield, of all teams, and another two League titles in 1931

OPPOSITE Herbert Chapman, the first great Arsenal manager

MIDDLE Herbert Chapman (centre), chats with a member of his team, Alex James (right), on the pitch at Wembley before the 1932 FA Cup Final

LEFT Bust of Herbert Chapman at Highbury

and 1933. They made it five in the decade, including three in a row in 1933-35, but Chapman died of pneumonia in 1934 age 55, having laid firm foundations for greatness. His bust was a talking point in the marble halls of Highbury, while such innovations as the white-sleeved kit live on.

Charity Shield

ARSENAL HAVE COMPETED in 19 FA Charity Shield finals since its 1908 inception, the first in 1930 when they beat Sheffield Wednesday 2-1. They went on to contest a further six before the 1930s finished. Victories in 1931, 1933, 1934 and 1938 did much to erase the disappointment of two defeats (1935 and 1936).

Arsenal again won the trophy in 1948 and 1953 but it would be over 40 years before they next claimed the Shield outright, having lost to Liverpool in 1979 and 1989.

FA Secretary Ted Croker proposed in 1974 that the Shield (renamed the FA Community Shield since 2001) should be played at Wembley as a curtain-raiser to the new season between the reigning League Champions and FA Cup holders.

The trophy was shared with arch-rivals Spurs following a 0-0 draw in 1991 and they lost a penalty shootout against Manchester United in 1993. Revenge was gained against the Old Trafford outfit, however with victories in 1998, 1999 and 2004.

Arsenal's 2002 victory over Liverpool was followed by defeat against Manchester United on pens (2003) and Chelsea (2005), the latter their fourth consecutive appearance. Only United and Liverpool have won the Shield more often.

RIGHT Tony Adams lifts the Charity Shield at Wembley, 1998

BELOW Gilberto celebrates after the Charity Shield win against Manchester United, 2004

Clichy

SIGNED BY ARSÈNE WENGER IN THE summer of 2003 from AS Cannes for £250,000, Gael Clichy (born in Toulouse, 26 July 1985) was the understudy to England international Ashley Cole until Cole left for Chelsea in August 2006. He had only played 15 games for Cannes, so was regarded as one for the future by the canny Arsène Wenger.

It seemed that Clichy, who made his debut against Rotherham in the Carling Cup in October 2003, would earn a regular first-team place in late 2005 when Cole broke his foot. All went well for six games, but by unlucky coincidence Clichy then suffered an identical injury to Cole while in action for the French Under-21 team. This also caused him to miss the end of the 2005-06 season including the Champions League Final.

He very nearly prevented Arsenal from reaching that stage, conceding a penalty in the final minute of the semi-final against Villarreal after returning from injury as a substitute. Goalkeeper Jens Lehmann saved Riquelme's penalty and Clichy suffered a recurrence of his injury in the match.

On the positive side, Clichy became the youngest winner of a Premiership medal when he earned this honour in his first season with Arsenal for his 12

BELOW Gael Clichy in action during the Premiership match against Bolton Wanderers, 2007

ABOVE Gael Clichy holds off the challenge of Yossi Benayoun of West Ham United

ABOVE RIGHT Ashley Cole, the man Clichy replaced

appearances in 2003-04.

Gael Clichy is now the first choice left-back at Arsenal, a position he claimed after appearing as a substitute against Watford in October 2006. Gael's pace, distribution and overlap-ping ability gives Arsenal strength in depth on the left and he remains a real prospect for the future. He made the full French squad for the first time in February 2007, a clear pointer to future honours.

Davis

ARSENAL'S DECISION TO GIVE PAUL Davis a free transfer in May 1995 ended a first-team career that spanned 15 fruitful years. The cultured midfielder, born on 9 December 1961 in London, had amassed an extensive medal collection that included two League Championships, two League Cups, the FA Cup and European Cup Winner's Cup.

Though absent through injury from Arsenal's title-clinching triumph at Anfield in 1989, Davis had been on the pitch two years earlier as Arsenal again beat Liverpool to win the Littlewoods Cup at Wembley. In 1991, he was involved in every game as Arsenal again won the title despite having two points deducted after a brawl at Manchester United.

Davis then fell from favour with manager George Graham, but although

he only played six League games in 1992-93 he appeared at Wembley three times as the Gunners became the first club to win both major domestic Cups in the same season. Sheffield Wednesday were the victims both times, although they took the FA Cup Final to a replay.

That success propelled Arsenal into the Cup Winners' Cup, where they beat Parma 1-0 in the Final. Davis scored, at Nottingham Forest in December 1994, signing off with a flourish in his 351st League game.

Derby Matches

THE FIRST EVER NORTH LONDON derby took place on 19 November 1887 when Tottenham Hotspur entertained Royal Arsenal on Tottenham Marshes. The home side, having been in existence five years longer than the infant Arsenal, won the tie 2-1. The first League game between the two sides occurred on

4 December 1909, a solitary Walter Lawrence strike giving Arsenal victory.

There have since been 155 competitive meetings between the two sides, with Arsenal holding the upper hand having won 65 times and drawn 41 games as shown in the following tables.

One of the most notable derbies was in 1968-69 when the two clubs were paired in a two-legged League Cup semifinal. Arsenal took a 1-0 advantage in the first leg, with John Radford scoring at Highbury. Although Jimmy Greaves put Spurs on level terms, Radford was again on target in the second leg and Arsenal won through to their second successive League Cup Final.

Spurs hosted Arsenal on 3 May 1971 for a Division One match with the visitors needing a score draw or better to claim the League title. An 86th-minute Ray Kennedy goal ensured the title was on its way to Highbury for the first time in almost 20 years and set up the first half of the Double.

The two sides met again in the semifinal of the Littlewoods (League) Cup in 1986-87 with Arsenal winning both legs by the same 2-1 margin to book their Wembley appearance.

They have also met in two FA Cup

semi-finals, both of which were played at Wembley. Spurs won the first encounter in April 1991 by a 3-1 margin but Arsenal exacted revenge two years later when Tony Adams scored the only goal of the game. The highest-scoring derby game took place on 13 November 2004 when Arsenal took the spoils in a 5-4 victory at White Hart Lane.

Alan Sunderland and Robert Pires jointly hold the record for scoring most against Spurs with eight apiece while David O'Leary holds the fixtures' appearance record, having played in 35 derby games between 1973-93.

League	P	W	D	L	F	A
Arsenal	140	57	38	45	210	188
Spurs	140	45	38	57	188	210
FA Cup	P	W	D	L	F	A
Arsenal	5	3	–	2	7	5
Spurs	5	2	–	3	5	7
League Cup	P	W	D	L	F	A
Arsenal	9	5	2	2	13	9
Spurs	9	2	2	5	9	13
Charity Shield	P	W	D	L	F	A
Arsenal	1	–	1	–	0	0
Spurs	1	–	1	–	0	0

Dial Square

THE ORIGINS OF ARSENAL FOOTBALL Club can be traced back to the formation of a works team in October 1886. This remained nameless for the first few weeks but it was eventually christened Dial Square FC because the majority of the team's first 15 players hailed from a workshop of the same name at the Royal Arsenal in Woolwich.

Dial Square, built in 1717, got its name from the large square sundial that was positioned over its entrance to the workshop in 1764. It survives into the 21st century and is cited by many as influencing the naming of the Clock End at Highbury.

David Danskin, one of the founder members, generously added three shillings (15p) out of his own pocket to the 6d (two-and-a-half pence) that was collected from each of the original 15 players. This fund was used to buy the club's first ever football.

Dial Square's inaugural match took place on 11 December 1886 when they beat Eastern Wanderers 6-0 on the Isle of Dogs, but the club's name was changed to Royal Arsenal two weeks later.

BELOW Arsenal team in front of the goal at the Clock End at Highbury 1971 - a reminder of Dial Square

Dixon

SIGNED FROM STOKE, AS WAS defensive colleague Steve Bould, in 1988, Manchester-born defender Lee Dixon (17 March 1964) proved great value for his £400,000 fee. But his early career looked unpromising, spells at Burnley, Chester and Bury leading to little.

After a near ever-present season at Gigg Lane he was on the move again, and it was at Stoke's Victoria Ground that he made his reputation. Known as the home of winger Stanley Matthews, the star performer was now a man that cut wingers down to size.

Lee missed the 1993 Coca-Cola Cup Final, but he bounced back to add an FA Cup winner's medal to two Championship medals and, after victory in Copenhagen, a '94 Cup Winners' Cup gong.

In international terms Dixon enjoyed his best period in 1990-93 when he made the England Number 2 shirt his own, having made his debut against Czechoslovakia. He scored his first and only international goal in a European Championship qualifier against Eire at Wembley in 1991, and

LEFT Dixon pictured during the Premiership match at Liverpool in 1999

amassed 21 caps in total.

Dixon continued to play at the highest level until 2002, when winning the Double for a second time provided the perfect finale to his career. Business ventures including running a restaurant have recently been augmented by a regular place among the Match Of The Day team of TV pundits for which his 815+22 career appearances (39 goals) makes him minently qualified.

Double

WHEN ARSENAL BAGGED THEIR third Double of League title and FA Cup in 2001-02, they equalled the record held by Manchester United. Prior to the Gunners' spectacular 1970-71 season, the only other club that had managed this feat in the 20th century was arch-rivals Spurs who claimed both trophies in 1960-61.

It was hardly an explosive start to 1970-71 season as Arsenal won two, drew two and lost one of the opening five games. The foundation for their success, however, was their home record as they dropped just three points at Highbury, winning 18 of their 21 games there. They lost a further five games away from home and claimed the trophy at White Hart Lane with a 1-0 victory.

They finished the season with 29 wins and seven draws from their 42 matches – with Ray Kennedy (20), John Radford (15) and George Graham (11) all hitting double figures – and overcame Liverpool 2-1 in a Wembley thriller.

The 1997-98 campaign was promising from the outset, with Arsenal remaining undefeated in the League until their visit to Derby County on 1 November where they lost 3-0. They endured a pre-Christmas stutter, losing three out of the next five games, but then went on an unbeaten run until the title had been clinched (the final two games away to Liverpool and Aston Villa saw 4-0 and 1-0 defeats respectively).

Their FA Cup Final opponents were a Newcastle United side who were contesting their first major final for 24 years but goals from Marc Overmars and Nicolas Anelka saw off the Magpies and brought the trophy to north London.

Arsenal's 2001-02 campaign would prove the opposite of their first Double season as although they lost just three games – all at home – they finished the season undefeated away from Highbury, winning 14 and drawing five matches to finish seven points ahead of second-placed Liverpool.

Their Cup Final opponents that year were Chelsea, who were appearing in the showpiece for the fourth time in nine years. Strikes from Ray Parlour and Freddie Ljungberg gave the Gunners victory over their London rivals and ensured that a third Double came to Highbury.

Arsenal also share another 'Double' record with Liverpool as they have both won the FA Cup and League Cup in the same season. The Highbury outfit achieved this in 1992-93 when they faced Sheffield Wednesday in both Finals. The League Cup was won by a 2-1 margin and, less than a month later, the two sides again met in the FA Cup. A 1-1 draw preceded Arsenal's 2-1 victory in the replay.

ABOVE Sam Bartram, the Charlton Athletic goalkeeper dives at the feet of Ted Drake during a match at Highbury in 1938

Drake

WHEN GEORGE ALLISON WAS FACED with the challenge of succeeding Herbert Chapman, his response was to make his first signing, from Southampton, a proven goalscorer. Ted Drake (born 16 August 1912) made an immediate impact, scoring on his debut against Wolverhampton Wanderers after his £6,500 move to Highbury in March 1934. He played too few games to qualify for a Championship medal, but 44 goals in the following season, also a title-winning campaign, established a club record that has endured into the current century.

But it was his feat the following term of scoring seven times in a single match that wrote worldwide headlines and ensured Ted Drake a place in the record books. The unfortunate opposition were Aston Villa, on their home ground, on 14 December 1935. An FA Cup in 1936 and League winner's medals in 1935 and 1938 were further evidence of his impact. But World War II foreshortened the success story, and a back injury caused his retirement in 1945. A total of 139 goals in 184 peacetime games told the tale, and he remains the club's fifth all-time top scorer. Five England appearances yielded six goals.

Ted Drake later managed Reading and Chelsea, guiding the latter to their first League Championship in 1955 (and their last until the Abramovich/Mourinho era). Surprisingly he didn't manage at this level again after leaving the Bridge in 1962, but had become the first player to win the League as both player and manager. He died in 1995.

European Cup

HAVING NOT WON THE LEAGUE Championship since 1952-53, Arsenal's first opportunity to compete against the best in Europe came courtesy of their 1970-71 Double.

Their inaugural campaign got off to a flying start with a 3-1 over Strømsgodset in Norway in September 1972. This was followed by a resounding 4-0 home victory in the second leg a fortnight later. The second round proved a formality as Grasshoppers Zurich were dispatched 5-0 on aggregate to set up a clash with holders Ajax.

The Dutch side provided a far sterner test, however, emerging from the first leg in Holland with a 2-1 advantage. The Gunners could not restore the balance in the second leg and, suffering a 1-0 reverse at Highbury, were knocked out of the competition by the eventual winners. Little did Arsenal suspect that it would be another 20 years before they qualified again (following the post-Heysel ban on English clubs).

FK Austria were the first round opponents in 1991-92 and Alan Smith scored four times at Highbury as the home side took a 6-1 advantage. Despite losing the return leg 1-0, Arsenal progressed to the second round where they faced Benfica. A 1-1 first leg draw in Portugal was a good result but it was Benfica who triumphed at Highbury winning 3-1 after extra time.

The competition has since been transformed into the Champions League.

ABOVE Benfica's Stefan Schwarz is challenged by Paul Davies, 1991

European Cup Winners' Cup

ARSENAL ONLY QUALIFIED FOR THE European Cup Winners' Cup three times and each time they reached the Final, winning just once before its 1998-99 demise.

The Gunners' 1993-94 campaign began and finished in Denmark. A 2-1 First Round first leg victory over OB Odense which was consolidated by a 1-1 draw in the return fixture. The Second Round saw them paired with Standard Liege and, following a 3-0 success in the home leg, Arsenal registered their biggest ever European win in Belgium as they completed a 7-0 rout.

A 0-0 home draw against Torino was followed by victory in Turin courtesy of a single Tony Adams goal which set up a semi-final clash with Paris St Germain. The away leg was drawn 1-1 and Sol Campbell scored the only goal of the return to secure Arsenal's place in the Final.

Alan Smith's strike half-way through the first half proved to be the only goal of the game against Parma in Copenhagen

and provided Arsenal's first European title in nearly a quarter of a century.

Their first appearance in 1979-80 saw them overcome Fenerbahce (Turkey) and FC Magdeburg (East Germany) to set up a quarter-final with IFK Gothenburg. The home leg was won 5-1 with Alan Sunderland bagging a brace prior to a goal-less draw in Sweden.

Italian giants Juventus were dispatched 2-1 on aggregate in the semis and Arsenal faced Valencia in Brussels for the trophy. The two sides fought out

BELOW Alan Smith of Arsenal holds the European Cup Winners' Cup aloft after beating Parma 1-0 in the Final, 1994

a 0-0 draw but the Spaniards broke Gunners' hearts with a 5-4 victory in the penalty shootout that followed.

Arsenal fans suffered similar heartache in 1994-95 as their heroes attempted to defend the trophy they had won the previous year.

Cypriot side Omonia Nicosia were beaten 6-1 on aggregate in the First Round with Brondby (Denmark) overcome by a 4-3 scoreline in the Second. An Ian Wright goal in each leg of the quarter-final against Auxerre gave the Highbury side a 2-1 aggregate victory and set up a meeting with Sampdoria. Steve Bould (2) and Wright gave Arsenal a 3-2 advantage to take to Italy but, with the score at 5-5 after extra time, the Italians succumbed 3-2 in the subsequent penalty shootout.

John Hartson cancelled out Esnaider's opening goal for Real Zaragoza in the Paris Final before former Spurs favourite Nayim outrageously shot from near the half-way line to catch David Seaman out of position and win the trophy in the last minute of extra time.

FA Cup

ARSENAL SHARE THE RECORD FOR the most FA Cup Final appearances (17) with Manchester United but lie one behind the Red Devils in terms of wins (11-10). They hold the record outright for the most semi-final appearances with 25, one ahead of United. Arsenal share another record with the Old Trafford side as they are only the second club to reach five successive semi-finals (2001-05).

The Gunners' first ever FA Cup fixture came on 5 October 1889 when they thrashed Lyndhurst 11-0 in a first round qualifier. Their first Final appearance came in 1927, the first time the country enjoyed a radio commentary of the match. Arsenal's Welsh keeper Dan Lewis stopped a Hugh Ferguson shot but, as he turned away from the oncoming forward, he knocked the ball into his own net for the only goal of the game.

The trophy was brought back to Highbury for the first time in 1930 following a 2-0 victory over Herbert Chapman's former club, Huddersfield Town, and the club appeared in two more Finals during that decade (losing 2-1 to Newcastle United in 1932 and beating Sheffield United 1-0 in 1936).

Two Final appearances in the 1950s saw mixed fortunes. Liverpool were beaten 2-0 in 1950 (without Arsenal ever having to leave the capital!) courtesy of two Reg Lewis goals, but two years later Newcastle United repeated the heartache of 20 years earlier with George Robledo scoring the only goal of the game as two Arsenal players lay injured seeking medical attention.

The 1970s brought two Cup Final victories and two defeats. Liverpool were beaten 2-1 in 1971 to secure the Double and a late Alan Sunderland goal gave

Arsenal a 3-2 triumph over Manchester United in 1979. Single-goal defeats were suffered by the Gunners in 1972 (against Leeds United), 1978 (Ipswich Town) and again in 1980 (West Ham United).

Having already beaten Sheffield Wednesday in the 1993 League Cup Final, the two sides met again in the FA Cup Final the following month. Goals from Ian Wright and Andy Linighan earned the Gunners a replay victory after the first game had ended one apiece.

Arsenal exacted revenge on Newcastle for their previous two Final defeats when they enjoyed a 2-0 victory over the Magpies in 1998 to secure a second Double before a repeat of the 1971 Final in 2001 at Cardiff's Millennium Stadium due to Wembley's redevelopment saw Liverpool triumph 2-1.

Cardiff was again the scene of jubilant celebrations as Arsenal claimed their third Double with a 2-0 victory over Chelsea in 2002. The Gunners returned the following year to register a 1-0 victory over Southampton and two years later emerged victorious from a penalty shootout after they had played out a goalless draw with Manchester United.

Famous Fans

THE LIST OF CELEBRITY FANS OF Arsenal is endless, but they include, from the music world: Natalie Appleton and Nicole Appleton (both ex All Saints); Dido; Judge Jules (DJ); Gary and Martin Kemp (the Spandau Ballet twins now turned actors); Johnny Rotten (Sex Pistols); Rachel Stevens (S Club 7); Margherita Taylor (DJ and presenter); Shovell (M People) and DJ Pete Tong.

Sporting celebrities include boxers Michael Watson, Nigel Benn and Audley Harrison; cricketer Phil Tufnell and Frankie Dettori (jockey). Greg Rusedski, the tennis ace is also a fan.

Arsenal also boasts a Royal follower, Prince Harry, as well as MP Kate Hoey and author Nick Hornby. Comedian Clive Anderson supports the Gunners as does Alan Davies (comedian and actor), Matt Lucas (Little Britain), Rory McGrath and Mel Smith. Actors who remain loyal (aside from the Kemp brothers) include: Lee McDonald (Zammo from *Grange Hill*); Andrew Paul and Erik Richard (*The Bill*); Joe Swash (*Eastenders*) and

Bradley Walsh (*Coronation Street*). Other celebrity fans include Jo Guest, Jeremy Beadle, Dale Winton and Dermot O'Leary.

RIGHT TOP Actor Alan Davies in the half time Celebrity Match at the Martin Keown Testimonial between Arsenal and England XI at Highbury in May 2004

RIGHT BELOW Presenter Dermot O'Leary

BELOW Jockey Frankie Dettori

George

ONE OF THE MOST FAMOUS OF ALL goal celebrations signalled more than just a winning goal at Wembley, it also cemented Arsenal's momentous Double of 1970-71. Charlie George, darling of the North Bank, thumped a 25-yarder into the back of the Liverpool net, and millions of TV viewers worldwide witnessed him savouring the moment by lying flat on his back with his arms outstretched

Born in Islington on 10 October 1950, Frederick Charles George was brought up in Tufnell Park and Camden Town and went to school in Holloway before signing for the Gunners in May 1966, making his first-team debut against Everton in August 1969. He stood out right away, having long, lank hair, a swagger borne of supreme confidence, plus bags of natural ability, whether playing in midfield or up front. He was

his own man in the dressing room, too, being famously up-front with his opinions. "I wasn't really a shy person," he once said, "and I always had plenty of confidence in my own ability."

Arsenal fans adored him: he was a local lad made good, Arsenal through and through, and supremely gifted.

ABOVE Charlie in action during a 1975 Division One match played at Highbury

Little wonder he was soon crowned King of Highbury.

Charlie played in both legs of Arsenal's 1970 Fairs Cup Final win over Anderlecht as the Gunners stormed back to win 4-3, and had his shirt ripped off his back by over-eager fans in the celebratory aftermath. However, he broke his ankle equalising against Everton in the opening match of the following campaign so had to sit out a chunk of the season. He was back for the fourth round tie with Portsmouth and scored in the replay as Arsenal won 3-2.

He netted twice in a 2-1 victory at Manchester City and scored the only goal in a sixth round replay against Leicester. He got lucky when a poor back pass contributed to Stoke taking a 2-0 lead in the semi-final, and it took a last-minute Storey penalty to earn a replay. Typically, he fired a long back pass to Bob Wilson early in the replay! A 2-0 win took the Gunners to Wembley.

After 179 matched for Arsenal, netting 49 goals, Charlie moved on to Derby (where he scored a European Cup hat-trick against Real Madrid), Southampton, Nottingham Forest, Bournemouth and Dundee, as well as spells in Australia, the United States and Hong Kong. He also gained a lone England cap. But he'll always be remembered for that Wembley moment.

Gillespie Road

GILLESPIE ROAD RUNS EAST-WEST along the north side of Highbury Stadium and is a hive of activity on matchdays with various stalls and an entrance to the North Bank Stand. Arsenal are the only football team in London with an Underground Station named after them and it is located here.

Opened as Gillespie Road on the Piccadilly Line in December 1906, the later arrival of the stadium led to a success-ful campaign for a change of name. On 31 October 1932 the station was renamed Arsenal (Highbury Hill) – the suffix has gradually been dropped over the years – but the original tiled walls of the platforms still bear the Gillespie Road name spelt out in large letters. The change meant that thousands of tickets, maps and signs had to be replaced.

It was Herbert Chapman who lobbied for the station to be re-christened. "Whoever heard of Gillespie Road?" he said at one point in the talks. "It is Arsenal around here!"

Pressure was growing to return the name to Gillespie Road as the club's move to the Emirates Stadium drew closer and an online petition was organised to lobby the Mayor of London, Ken Livingstone.

BELOW Fans outside Arsenal tube station after a match

Graham

GEORGE GRAHAM WILL FOREVER be linked to Arsenal. As a player, 'Stroller' was as stylish for the Gunners as he was successful, and when he

returned as manager he turned the club into one of the leading forces of the late 1980s and early '90s. But for all his achievements at Highbury, Graham will also be remembered as the manager who was caught 'taking a bung'.

Born in Bargeddie, Scotland, on 30 November 1944, George Graham joined Aston Villa in December 1961 but after only a handful of games moved on to Chelsea in 1964. He won a League Cup winner's medal in 1965 with the Blues but a year later he joined Arsenal for £50,000. He was soon a key member of the side, although he had to make do with just a couple of League Cup runners-up medals in 1968 and 1969.

Then it all came good: in 1970 he helped Arsenal win Inter-Cities Fairs Cup, overcoming Anderlecht in a two-legged final and he was a pivotal player as Arsenal stormed to the League and Cup Double in 1970-71. A move to Manchester United ensued in 1972 and he later had spells for Portsmouth and Crystal Palace before hanging up his boots in 1977. Coaching jobs at QPR and Crystal Palace paved the way for a first managerial job at Millwall in 1982. Four years later he took over the Arsenal hot seat from Don Howe.

It was to be an eventful few seasons on many levels. The former midfield schemer turned his focus on making Arsenal a difficult team to beat and before long "1-0 to the Arsenal" became a terrace chant on the back of a string of ground-out victories. Not that Gunners fans were unduly bothered: Graham's regular back four of Tony Adams, Steve Bould, Nigel Winterburn and Lee Dixon would go on to attain legendary status, while the tactics took Arsenal to the top and reaped a stack of silverware.

In eight seasons under Graham Arsenal won two League Championships, two League Cups, an FA Cup and the European Cup Winners' Cup. The 1989 Championship, Arsenal's first for 18 years, was only secured thanks to Michael Thomas's last-gasp winner at Anfield, but in 1990-91 Arsenal lost only one League match all season although they were deducted two points following an on-pitch brawl at Old Trafford. Captain Tony Adams, meantime, was jailed for 56 days for drink-driving.

Unfortunately, there was more controversy to come in late 1994 – first, Paul Merson rocked the club with his drink and drugs confessions, then Graham himself was accused of taking a bung in the transfer of John Jensen. In February 1995 he was sacked by Arsenal and was banned from football for a year. He went on to manage Leeds and Spurs, but is now a TV pundit.

BELOW Graham the manager holds the trophy as the team parade in North London after winning the 1994 European Cup Winners' Cup

Greatest XI

Manager
Arsène Wenger

1	David Seaman
2	Pat Rice
3	Ashley Cole
4	Patrick Vieira
5	Frank McLintock
6	Tony Adams
7	Liam Brady
8	Thierry Henry
9	Ted Drake
10	Dennis Bergkamp
11	Cliff Bastin

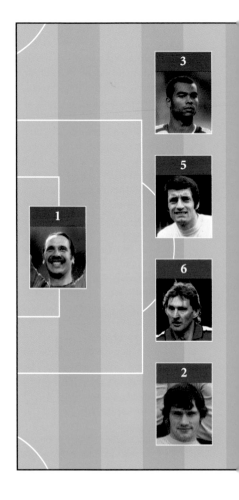

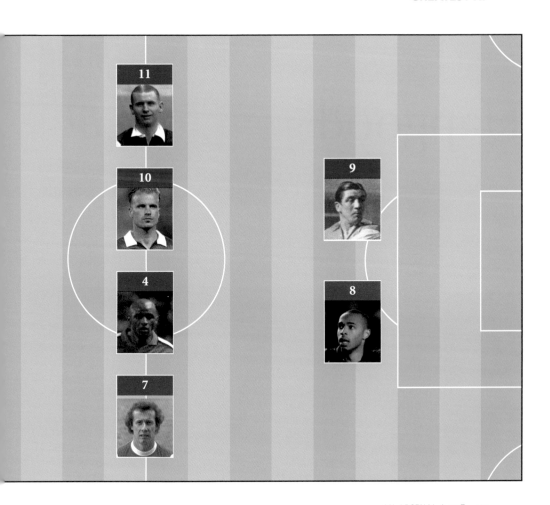

Hapgood

ORIGINALLY A MILKMAN, EDRIS Albert ('Eddie') Hapgood played as an amateur before getting a break at Kettering Town. Born on 24 September 1908, he was signed to Arsenal for £950 by Herbert Chapman in 1927 – an astute buy which helped to seal a reputation as one of the all-time greats in football management for Chapman.

Hapgood made 393 League appearances for Arsenal, winning five Championship medals and two FA Cup winner's medals. He became a household name as captain of both Arsenal and England – at a time when both sides dominated the game – and his sporting achievements are legendary. As left-back, he was widely recognised as one of the few defenders able to play opposite Stanley Matthews.

Hapgood played 30 times for England and wore the captain's armband 21 times.

He made his international debut on 13 May 1933 against Italy in Rome, unfortunately kicking the ball into the lap of the Italian dictator Benito Mussolini. His first international as captain was also against Italy, then World Champions, at Highbury on 14 November 1934 in the Battle of Highbury.

His worst moment came on 14 May 1938 where, under pressure from British diplomats, Hapgood and his team gave the Nazi salute before a match against Germany in Berlin. England went on to win the match 6-3.

World War II brought a premature end to his professional career, but Eddie went on to be manager at Blackburn (1944-47) and Watford (1948-50) before his death on 20 April 1973.

Henry

WHEN THIERRY HENRY (BORN IN Paris of West Indian parentage on 17 August 1977) came to Highbury in 1999 for a reported fee of £10.5 million, he had already helped Monaco to the French First Division title and his country to the World Cup. A move to Juventus saw things go wrong for this graduate of the French national academy, 3 goals in 16 appearances hardly impressing.

Arsène Wenger had worked with Henry when manager of Monaco, and saw the potential of converting the winger into a striker. A bid of £10.5 million was accepted, and subsequent events proved this to be a bargain. By the time Arsenal won the Double in 2002 Henry was the Premiership's top scorer with 24, having meanwhile helped his country win Euro 2000 with three goals. The Champions League proved a challenge he was more than capable of meeting, seven goals in 12 games his first offering.

ABOVE Henry celebrates after scoring against Middlesbrough at the Emirates in 2006

RIGHT Captain Henry celebrates a 1-0 aggregate win in the Champions League semi-final against Villarreal in April 2006

BELOW Henry shoots for goal during the Premiership match against Charlton, 2005

Henry's turn of speed, close control and reading of the game make him the perfect all-round striker. He is also a creator of goals, as the likes of Pires, Ljungberg, Bergkamp and Reyes would attest. His temperament has occasionally been suspect, a sending off in the 2002 World Cup against Uruguay a rare black mark. But marriage and fatherhood tamed even that, and by 2006 he had overtaken all previous records to stand as not only Arsenal's all-time leading marksman but also the Premiership's third highest goalscorer.

His goal feats are prodigious. He became the first player to retain the European Golden Boot in 2005, while the same year saw him pass Ian Wright's record haul of 185. The following year saw him beat Cliff Bastin's previously unparalleled 151 League goals, while he became the first player to score a century at Highbury. He has achieved equal notoriety in polls of players and football writers, having been PFA Player of the Year twice and the French Player of the Year a record four times. 2006 saw him the writers' choice yet again. Henry suc-ceeded Patrick Vieira as captain in 2005 on his countryman's departure to Juventus, but he leads more by example than exhortation. Even this, though, failed to persuade him to commit his future to the club and transfer talk abounded in 2006 as the Gunners prepared for their move to Ashburton Grove: popular rumour had it that he would wait the outcome of the Champions League Final before committing himself.

Henry finally departed Arsenal in the summer of 2007 for Barcelona.

Highbury

PRIOR TO MOVING TO HIGHBURY, Arsenal played their home games at the Manor Ground on Plumstead Common and the last match there – a 1-1 draw with Middlesbrough – took place on 26 April 1913.

Henry Norris was the man who instigated the move and he had a financial interest in both Arsenal and Fulham at the time. Having saved Arsenal from bankruptcy in 1910, the League rejected his plans of first a merger and then a groundshare with Fulham and Norris eventually concluded that the club would have to relocate if they were to prosper in the capital.

With sites at Battersea and Haringey being rebuffed, Norris decided on land belonging to St John's Divinity College in Avenell Road. Despite objections from local residents and neighbouring clubs, including Spurs and Leyton Orient, the League Management Committee gave

sides featured banked terracing.

The West Stand, with a distinctive Art Deco style, was opened in 1932 by Prince Edward and Leitch's main stand was demolished in 1936 to make way for a new East stand matching the West one. The terraces at the north and south ends were both given roofs, and the southern terrace had a clock fitted to its front, giving it the name Clock End.

Little changed at Highbury until the Taylor Report on the Hillsborough disaster was published, recommending that stadiums become all-seater. This work was rapidly completed, giving a capacity of 38,500. This was substantially smaller than some of their Premiership rivals so the club agreed to construct a replacement nearby, the new Emirates Stadium, to be completed in time for the 2006-07 campaign.

As well as being home to Arsenal, 12 England internationals were played at Highbury from 1920-61 and 12 FA Cup semi-finals as a neutral ground (1929-97). Highbury has also seen several cricket and baseball matches, and was the venue for the 1966 World Heavyweight boxing title bout between Henry Cooper and

the go-ahead for the proposal.

Norris paid a then-astronomical fee of £20,000 for a 21-year lease that stipulated no games could be played on Good Friday or Christmas Day, an arrangement that continued until the land was bought outright in 1925.

Designed by renowned football architect Archibald Leitch, the new stadium featured a single stand on the eastern side with the nine gables spelling out ARSENAL FC, while the other three

Howe

DONALD HOWE (BORN 12 OCTOBER 1935) spent most of his playing career at West Bromwich Albion, making his debut in 1955. He became an England regular, playing in the 1958 World Cup and winning 23 caps.

Signed for Arsenal in 1964 by Billy Wright, he was a well-respected player but he broke his leg against Blackpool in 1966 and was unable to play in the first team again. Howe retired and went on to become a respected coach and manager.

He became Arsenal's reserve-team coach under Bertie Mee and in 1968, after the departure of Dave Sexton, he stepped up to the first team.

Arsenal won the Double in 1971, but he decided to return to his old club, West Bromwich Albion, as manager. This was not a successful move and the club were relegated to Division Two in 1973.

He had spells as coach with Galatasaray, Turkey and Leeds before returning to Arsenal in 1977 as head coach under manager Terry Neill. In December 1983, Howe became manager but success eluded him and he resigned in March 1986.

After further management spells, Howe moved into journalism and broadcasting before returning to coach England in the mid-1990s under Terry Venables. He returned to Arsenal a second time in 1997 as a youth-team coach. He has a regular column in Arsenal's official magazine and still runs youth coaching schemes.

ABOVE Don Howe in action, 1966

Internationals

BY THE START OF 2006, A TOTAL OF 53 Arsenal players had represented England. Seven of these – Frank Moss, George Male, Eddie Hapgood, Wilf Copping, Ray Bowden, Ted Drake and Cliff Bastin – were in the same team that faced World Cup holders Italy on 14 November 1934 at Highbury. An inexperienced England (with every player having less than ten caps for his country) won 3-2 in a hotly contested and frequently violent match that became known as the Battle of Highbury.

Billed in England as the 'real' World Cup Final, because the English FA had withdrawn from FIFA so the national side had not competed in the Finals, the match meant so much to the Italians that Benito Mussolini reportedly offered each player an Alfa Romeo car and the equivalent of £150 if they won.

Highbury's hallowed turf was graced by a trio of World Cup winners following the 1998 Finals in France. Midfielders Patrick Vieira and Emmanuel Petit (scorer of the second goal in the Final against Brazil) and striker Thierry Henry all returned from their homeland proudly displaying their medals. Brazilian midfielder Gilberto also claimed a World Cup winner's medal, having played every minute of his country's 2002 tournament.

The players who have won the most caps for their country during their time at Arsenal (to June 2007):

Player	Country	Caps
Thierry Henry	FRA	82
Patrick Vieira	FRA	78
Kenny Sansom	ENG	77
David Seaman	ENG)	72
David O'Leary	IRL	68
Tony Adams	ENG	66
Pat Rice	NIR	49
Sammy Nelson	NIR	48
Terry Neill	NIR	44
Sylvain Wiltord	FRA	44
Pat Jennings	NIR	42

Other notable Arsenal players who have impressed on the international scene include Jack Kelsey and Dave Bowen, part of the Wales side who reached the quarter-finals of the 1958 World Cup before losing to eventual winners Brazil.

A number of Arsenal players have captained their country including David Jack, George Male, Eddie Hapgood, Alan Ball, David Platt, Tony Adams, David Seaman and Martin Keown (all England); Dave Bowen (Wales); Nwankwo Kanu (Nigeria) and Patrick Vieira (France).

The Gunners' Premiership clash against Birmingham City on 2 October 2005 was designated as Internationals Day – one of many themed matchdays to commemorate the club's final season at Highbury – and spectators could watch footage of Arsenal's international stars on the giant screen.

BELOW French midfielder Patrick Vieira during the World Cup qualifying match against Cyprus, 2005

Jack

CULTURED MIDFIELDER DAVID Jack became the first ever £10,000 footballer when he was signed by Herbert Chapman from Bolton Wanderers in 1928. The fee of £10,890 more than doubled the previous record. Intended to replace the gifted but ageing Charles Buchan, inside-forward Jack (born 3 April 1899) more than repaid the fee with 208 first-class appearances, in which he notched an impressive 124 goals, including a semi-final winner in 1930 that helped the Gunners on their way to their first ever FA Cup win. He remains today in the Top 10 of Gunners goalscorers.

The son of Scottish footballer and manager Bob Jack, David began his career with Plymouth, the club his father had managed, before the Trotters returned him to the town of his birth via a £3,500 bid in 1920. He achieved much in eight seasons at Bolton, including the first FA Cup Final goal at Wembley in 1923. Surprisingly he only achieved nine England caps, scoring three times.

Jack retired in 1934 with three Championship medals in his collection, but continued in the game as manager of Southend United (1934-40), where his father, who scouted for him, had previously been boss, and Middlesbrough (1944-52). He died in 1958.

Jennings

PAT JENNINGS, BORN IN NEWRY, Northern Ireland on 12 June 1945, chose soccer over Gaelic football to become a London footballing legend. After one season with Watford, during which he won the first of an amazing 119 Northern Irish caps, he moved to White Hart Lane where he played some 590 League and Cup matches.

His move to Highbury came in the summer of 1977, after Spurs had finished bottom of Division One, then the top flight. At 32, he was perhaps considered past his best, but Gunners fans quickly forgot his previous association as he helped Arsenal to three FA Cup Finals (one won) and one European Cup Winners' Cup Final. A bargain for a fee of £45,000.

Internationally, the large-handed Jennings was the other world-class player in the Northern Ireland side alongside George Best. Overtaking Terry Neill's record of 59 caps in 1976, he went on to more than double that number and grace the 1982 World Cup Finals.

Agile, fearless and with a massive kick that led, on one occasion, to a goal,

Jennings was awarded the OBE shortly after his retirement in 1985. The football writers' Player of the Year in 1973, he is that rarity in north London football – a legend at both Arsenal and Spurs.

ABOVE Pat Jennings in goal for Arsenal

Kelsey

ALFRED JOHN 'JACK' Kelsey, born in Swansea on 19 November 1929, distinguished himself as keeper for both Arsenal and Wales, exceeding 300 League appearances for the Gunners and obtaining 41 international caps.

He was working as the village blacksmith when, in August 1949, Arsenal signed him from local side Winch Wen as reserve to George Swindin. A League Championship medal was won in 1952-53, with Swindin injured for much of that campaign, after which Kelsey became an automatic choice for club and country. His physical presence in an era when keepers were not protected as today, combined with agility, made him one of the best of his day even if Arsenal's form was often indifferent.

Kelsey more than played his part in helping Wales to the World Cup quarter-finals in 1958 where a deflected shot from Pelé took Brazil one step closer to the trophy. The Brazilians, impressed, referred to him as 'the cat with magnetic paws'. Ironically, the back injury that ended his international career was sustained in a friendly in Rio in 1962. Kelsey retired from League football shortly afterwards, but stayed on as Arsenal's club-shop (and later commercial) manager until 1989. He died in March 1992, aged 62.

Kennedy

BORN IN NORTHUMBERLAND ON 28 July 1951, Ray Kennedy formed a prolific forward partnership with John Radford in Arsenal's Double-winning team. He notched 36 goals in that season, including the winner against Spurs that clinched the League title. This was all the sweeter since he had been rejected when a youngster by lowly Port Vale. His first notable contribution to Arsenal history had come as a goalscoring sub in the 1969 Fairs Cup (now UEFA Cup) Final against Anderlecht, which the club won.

He followed his Double season in which he missed just one match with a 26-goal haul in 1971-72 but was only a sub when the Gunners returned to Wembley to lose to Leeds. Two more seasons brought no more medals, but his next move would help him complete the set.

Ray's transfer to Anfield in 1974 for a £180,000 fee was the last act of Liverpool's legendary manager Bill Shankly. His successor Bob Paisley, blessed with the Keegan-Toshack combination up front, gave Kennedy a new lease of life by converting him to a midfielder, and he won 17 England caps in that role. He also played a key role in Liverpool's European domination of the time.

Sadly, he was stricken by Parkinson's disease after joining Swansea in 1982, but since his retirement has pluckily spent time fundraising in an attempt to find a cure.

BELOW Ray Kennedy, 1971

Kits

ARSENAL'S FIRST STRIP WAS donated by Nottingham Forest after founder member Fred Beardsley wrote to them advising that his fledgling outfit could not afford to kit themselves out. His former club responded by supplying a complete set of long-sleeved dark red shirts with three buttons down the front and a ball.

Arsenal have been associated with red ever since (despite a brief flirtation with the addition of thin blue vertical stripes in 1895) and the white sleeves were added by Herbert Chapman for a home match against Liverpool on 4 March 1933.

Chapman also decided to incorporate the club badge into the kit and it was positioned on the left-hand side of the shirt.

In the 1950s, a second kit was introduced to be used away from Highbury to avoid any clash of colours with opposing teams wearing similar kits. A gold ensemble was worn for the first time in the 1950 FA Cup Final meeting with Liverpool.

Other notorious away kits include yellow for a 1953 FA Cup tie with Blackpool, 1982-83's green shirts with blue sleeves and 1992's off-yellow that has often been described as looking like bruised bananas.

In 1960, Arsenal moved away from the woven rugby shirt style to a new

knitted cotton jersey as new technologies improved. The club also returned to a plain red shirt early in this decade but the arrival of Bertie Mee as manager saw the reinstatement of the white sleeves.

The famous cannon graphic appeared on the shirt for the first time in the early 1970s and it was in this shirt that Arsenal won the Double in 1970-71 while the end of the decade saw the shirt featuring a kit manufacturers' logo for the first time, in this case Umbro.

JVC became the Club's first shirt sponsor in 1982, replaced by SEGA in 1999 and O2 in 2002. From 2006-07 the sponsors will be Fly Emirates in a deal lasting eight years.

ABOVE Ljungberg in the 2001-02 gold away kit

LEFT Wright in the outrageous away kit worn from 1991 to 1993

FAR LEFT Cole wearing the 2002-03 away kit featuring a geometric print on the front

In their final Highbury season, Arsenal dropped the white sleeves and created a 'redcurrant' shirt with gold lettering to honour that worn in the first season at the ground.

Lambert

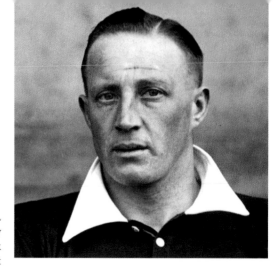

SIGNED FOR ARSENAL for £2,000 in June 1926 by Herbert Chapman, Jack Lambert was a robust centre-forward born on 22 May 1902. He began his career for Rotherham County and played in just one Division Two game for Leeds United before being released to Doncaster Rovers. It was here that he came to prominence after becoming a regular goalscorer for the club.

Lambert struggled at Arsenal, scoring only once in his first season. He was forced to play understudy to Jimmy Brain for several years, but finally made a breakthrough during the 1929-30 season when he scored 18 goals in 20 appearances with the aid of Alex James. He also scored Arsenal's first goal in the FA Cup Final victory over Huddersfield in 1930, giving the club its first major trophy.

The following season was even better for Lambert when he scored 38 League goals (a club record – later broken by Ted Drake) that included seven hat-tricks. Arsenal went on to win the First Division title that season.

Lambert played for Arsenal for the next few years, scoring regularly (including five goals in a 9-2 defeat over Sheffield United). The Gunners again won the First Division title in 1933.

In October 1933, Arsenal's signing of Jimmy Dunne saw Lambert sold to Fulham where he played for two seasons before retiring in 1935. He returned to Arsenal as a coach for the reserve side, but was tragically killed in a car accident on 7 December 1940, aged 38.

League Championship

WOOLWICH ARSENAL WERE LON-don's only professional club when they joined the newly-extended Football League in 1893 and they finished ninth out of 15 in their first Second Division campaign. They have since won ten First Division titles.

The Gunners won promotion to the First Division as runners-up in 1904, mainly due to their home record where they scored 67 goals and only conceded five. Never finishing higher than sixth, they remained in the top flight until 1913 when they suffered their only ever relegation. They returned to the top flight in mysterious circumstances with the resumption of League Football after the First World War and have remained there ever since – a record no other club can match.

The glory era began following the arrival of manager Herbert Chapman and five League titles were won in the 1930s. Arsenal equalled the record of Huddersfield Town, Chapman's former club, between 1924-26 by winning a hat-

trick of back-to-back titles themselves (1933-35) to go alongside their 1930-31 and 1937-38 Championships. Liverpool (1982-86) and Manchester United (1999-2001) have since equalled that feat.

With the onset of the Second World War, it was another ten years before Arsenal again won the First Division but when they won their next title five years later they did so with the lowest points

ABOVE Thomas defeats Grobbelaar of Liverpool during the infamous match at Anfield in 1989

total ever. The Gunners and Preston amassed just 54 points from 42 games, but the trophy went to Highbury on goal average.

As mentioned previously, Arsenal became only the second club to achieve the Double in the 20th century when they won the First Division at White Hart Lane in May 1971.

There was a major change in the Football League in 1981-82 when the number of points for a victory was increased from two to three in a bid to encourage teams to be more adventurous.

The 1988-89 campaign saw a nail-biting finish, Arsenal having to go to Liverpool and win by two goals to claim the title and avoid the Merseysiders being crowned Champions. Alan Smith scored after 52 minutes but it was Michael Thomas who sent the fans delirious when he netted the vital second goal 86 seconds into injury time.

The 1990-91 First Division title was Arsenal's last before the formation of the Premiership and they finished seven points clear of Liverpool despite being fined two points for a brawl at Old Trafford that had included nearly all 22 players (United were fined one point for their part in the fracas).

League Cup

ARSENAL FIRST ENTERED THE League Cup in 1966-67 as the competition was in its seventh year. Needing two replays to overcome Third Division Gillingham, the Gunners' first campaign ended in a 3-1 defeat at home to West Ham in the Third Round.

The following season took them all the way to a Wembley meeting with Leeds United. The Yorkshire side triumphed with a goal from full-back Terry Cooper to earn the club's first ever trophy.

Arsenal fought their way to a second successive Final appearance in 1968-69, against Third Division Swindon Town. Roger Smart scored first for the unfancied Wiltshire side on 34 minutes following a mix-up between Ure and Wilson but Bobby Gould equalised four minutes from time. Unfortunately, the heavy conditions and the flu virus that had been doing the rounds of Highbury took its toll on the First Division outfit and Swindon's Don Rogers scored twice in extra time.

Arsenal had to wait another 18 years to reach the Final again, against a Liverpool side who had won the trophy four times in the previous six years.

ABOVE Portrait of David Rocastle posing with the Littlewoods Cup

Prolific Welsh striker Ian Rush, in his last Liverpool appearance at Wembley before his transfer to Juventus, opened the scoring after 23 minutes when he latched onto Craig Johnston's pass.

Scottish striker Charlie Nicholas equalised just as half-time approached and it was Arsenal who piled on the

pressure after the interval. It was Nicholas again, fed by Perry Groves, who sent the Highbury faithful into raptures when he netted his second seven minutes from time with a deflected shot that left Bruce Grobbelaar stranded.

Arsenal found themselves at Wembley again the following year, facing Luton Town. It was the underdogs who took the lead first when Brian Stein scored after 15 minutes to shock the Gunners. Martin Hayes equalised in the second half and, when Alan Smith scored five minutes later, it looked like the trophy would be heading back to Highbury.

The Hatters, however, had other ideas and – after Nigel Winterburn had missed the chance to put Arsenal 3-1 up from the penalty spot – Danny Wilson equalised with just five minutes on the clock. In the dying seconds, Stein latched onto Ashley Grimes' pass to score his second and Luton's third of the game.

Arsenal's most recent appearances were in 1993, when they beat Sheffield Wednesday 2-1, and in 2007 when they lost 2-1 to Chelsea in a bad-tempered match with dismissals on both sides. Adebayor and Toure both walked in the final minute.

Lehmann

IT HAS BEEN SAID YOU HAVE to be a bit off the wall to be a goalkeeper, and that holds true with Gunners shot-stopper Jens Lehmann. Confident, physical and aggressive, the German arrived at Highbury in the summer of 2003 with the task of filling David Seaman's large gloves. After a Community Shield loss against Manchester United in his debut, it would be over a year before he again tasted defeat in a domestic match.

Born on 10 November 1969, Lehmann began his professional career aged 20 with FC Schalke 04 in the Bundesliga, helping them win the UEFA Cup in 1997. That led to a big move to Italian giants AC Milan, where he unfortunately didn't realise his potential, and only played a handful of games. A return to his homeland beckoned with Borussia Dortmund, where Lehmann won the Bundesliga in 2002.

Competition clearly brings out the best in the German international. A few mistakes in the 2004-05 season saw manager Arsène Wenger experiment with Manuel Almunia. When the Spaniard could not keep his place, Lehmann seized the opportunity with both hands, culminating in a man of the match performance in Arsenal's FA Cup Final victory over Manchester United. A last-minute penalty save against Villarreal that took the Gunners to the 2006 Champions League Final only endeared him further to the Highbury faithful.

Lehmann's well-publicised rivalry with fellow German goalkeeper Oliver Kahn saw both men play alternate matches in the lead-up to the 2006 World Cup, Jens emerging as first choice.

Ljungberg

FIERY ATTACKING MIDFIELDER Freddie Ljungberg enjoys 'veteran' status at Highbury – a term that is becoming less frequent in an increasingly young Gunners side. Make no mistake however, this 'old-timer' (born 16 April 1977) has still got plenty left in his tank. Though not as prolific in front of goal in recent seasons, Freddie still contributes through his assists and continuous attacking threat, be it through the middle or up the right flank.

Currently the longest-serving Arsenal player with the departure of Dennis Bergkamp, Ljungberg has played nearly 300 appearances for the Gunners, scoring over 60 goals in that time.

Manager Arsène Wenger signed

Ljungberg in the summer of 1998 without ever scouting the player in person; a noticeable performance in Sweden's international victory over England confirmed reports that had already reached Wenger, and a fee of £3 million was agreed with Swedish side Halmstads BK. Freddie went on to score on his debut against Manchester United after less than five minutes on the pitch - not a bad way to announce your arrival in the English game.

Most fans will remember the tail end of the 2001-02 season as perhaps Ljungberg's greatest run in the Arsenal side. His run of seven goals in seven games – including a Cup Final goal against Chelsea – helped Arsenal clinch the Premiership and FA Cup double and consequently earned Freddie the Barclaycard Player of the Year award. In the year that he would come to prominence, not least for the trend-setting red streak in his hair, Ljungberg also picked up the Swedish Player of the Year award – the Guldbollen. Unfortunately a hip complaint limited his World Cup appearances that summer in Japan, a tournament many believed he could have used to make his mark on the world scale.

Macdonald

BORN IN FULHAM ON 7 JANUARY 1950, bandy-legged Malcolm 'Supermac' Macdonald made his League debut for his local league team as an 18-year-old. But though he was successfully transformed from full-back to striker, he departed to Luton in the summer of 1969 to register more than a goal every two games over two seasons. From there he moved to Newcastle in 1971 for £180,000 to fill the iconic Number 9 shirt with success. 'Supermac' became a Tyneside legend, and in spring 1975 followed a goal against World Cup holders Germany with all five against Cyprus, equalling an England record (he would end up with 14 caps and one further goal.)

He signed for Arsenal in 1976 for £333,333, the first major acquisition of Terry Neill's managerial reign. He top-scored in both his first two seasons at Highbury. But a knee injury at the start of the 1978-79 season spelled the end to his career, though he briefly tried to play on in the less taxing Swedish league. Returning to Fulham in a business-related role, Macdonald switched to manager but after a promising start with promotion to Division Two (now the Championship) in 1982 it all went wrong. He now combines after-dinner speaking with radio punditry on Tyneside, where he continues to be revered.

Managers

Sam Hollis
August 1894-July 1897

Thomas Mitchell
August 1897-March 1898

George Elcoat
March 1898-May 1899

Harry Bradshaw
August 1899-May 1904

Phil Kelso
July 1904-February 1908

George Morrell
February 1908-May 1915

Leslie Knighton
May 1919-June 1925

Herbert Chapman
June 1925-January 1934

Joe Shaw*
January 1934-June 1934

George Allison
June 1934-May 1947

Tom Whittaker
June 1947-October 1956

Jack Crayston
October 1956-May 1958

George Swindin
June 1958-May 1962

Billy Wright
May 1962-June 1966

Bertie Mee
June 1966-May 1976

Terry Neill
July 1976-December 1983

Don Howe
December 1983- March 1986

ABOVE Billy Wright, the new manager of Arsenal, directs a training session in 1962

MANAGERS

Steve Burtenshaw*
March 1986-May 1986

George Graham
May 1986-February 1995

Stewart Houston*
February 1995-June 1995

Bruce Rioch
June 1995-August 1996

Stewart Houston*
August 1996-September 1996

Pat Rice*
September 1996

Arsène Wenger
September 1996-date

* = temporary appointment

BELOW Arsene Wenger shakes hands with fans after the last Premiership match at Highbury

McLintock

GLASGOW-BORN FRANK McLINT-
ock (born 28 December 1939) signed
for Leicester City on his 17th birthday
in January 1957 after a week-long trial,
and went on to play more than 150
League games for the club, making two
unsuccessful FA Cup Final appearances,
in 1961 and 1963, and having a League
Cup Final outing – and another runners-up medal – in 1964, before being
transferred to Arsenal in October 1964.

Manager Billy Wright shelled out a
then British record fee of £80,000 for
the commanding wing-half. By 1967 he
was club captain. Two further League
Cup Finals defeats, to Leeds and
Swindon, contributed to him putting in
a transfer request. Bertie Mee, his manager by then, talked him out of moving,
while his sidekick Don Howe was
instrumental in Frank switching to the
heart of the defence.

In his next Cup Final outing, in 1970
McLintock gained a winner's medal in
dramatic circumstances. After losing the
first leg of the Fairs Cup final 3-1 to
Anderlecht, McLintock skippered his
side to a 3-0 triumph at Highbury. A

ABOVE Inspirational Gunners skipper Frank McLintock

model of consistency, he missed just one
of Arsenal's 64 games during that campaign. The following season Arsenal
made a bold assault on the First Division
Championship and the FA Cup – with
captain McLintock ever-present at centre-half.

ABOVE Frank McLintock of Arsenal in action during a match against Leeds at Highbury in 1970

Arsenal secure a famous League and Cup Double by beating Liverpool 2-1 at Wembley and McLintock could forget his previous Wembley disappointments by triumphantly holding the trophy aloft. To crown his season, McLintock's part in the notable double was duly acknowledged when he was named Footballer of the Year.

By the time McLintock led his side back to Wembley in 1972, where they were pipped by Leeds, he'd been awarded an MBE. In 1972-73 Arsenal couldn't catch Liverpool and were First Division runners-up. A move to Queens Park Rangers ensued and in 1976 he almost led them to the title, but Liverpool won a close contest. After retiring in May 1977 – having racked up more than 600 League games in all and picking up nine Scottish caps – McLintock returned to Leicester as manager. He later managed Brentford before turning his attentions to media punditry.

It all came to a head in the first week of May 1971. On a pulsating Monday evening at, of all places, White Hart Lane, Arsenal saw off Spurs with a single Ray Kennedy goal to clinch the championship. The following weekend Charlie George's majestic extra-time strike saw

McNab

ROBERT McNAB (BORN 20 JULY 1943) began his career with his local club, Huddersfield Town, but was signed for Arsenal by Bertie Mee in October 1966. He immediately won a place on the first team and was first-choice left-back for the next nine seasons, gracing the 1968 and 1969 League Cup Finals.

During a career that spanned 18 years, his form and success at the north London club inspired England manager Alf Ramsey to select him on four occasions, making his debut against Romania in 1968. Despite not becoming a regular for the national side, McNab enjoyed success at home, winning the Inter-Cities Fairs Cup (1970) and the Double in 1971.

Although he continued to play for the Gunners through much of the early 1970s, the arrival of Sammy Nelson and a career blighted with injuries meant that McNab was no longer guaranteed a place on the first team. He was released on a free transfer in 1975 and he went on to play for Wolves before moving to the US to play in the NASL

for San Antonio (Texas).

Shortly before retiring he played for non-league Barnet before taking up a coaching position with the Vancouver Whitecaps. He lives in to Los Angeles, California where he is a property developer.

BELOW Gritty Yorkshireman Bob McNab

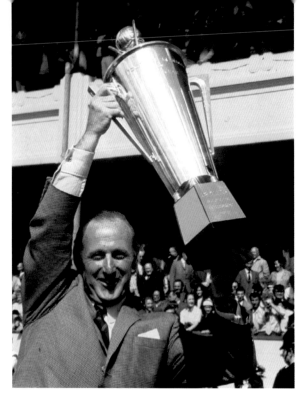

Mee

BORN ON 25 DECEMBER 1918 IN Bulwell, Nottingham, Bertie Mee played as winger for Derby County in 1938 and Mansfield Town in 1939 during his early days but his playing career was cut short by injury.

He joined the Royal Army Medical Corps where he trained as a physiotherapist and spent six years rising to the rank of sergeant. After working at various football clubs as a physiotherapist, Mee succeeded Billy Milne at Arsenal in 1960.

After the sacking of Billy Wright, Mee surprisingly became manager in June 1966. Perhaps this move was totally unexpected as he asked for a 'get-out' clause in his contract allowing him to return to being a physiotherapist after 12 months if things didn't work out. In a shrewd move, he also recruited Dave Sexton and Don Howe as assistants to make up for any tactical shortcomings of his own.

It was 13 years since Arsenal had won a trophy, but under the guidance of Mee – with players from the 1966 FA Youth Cup-winning side including Charlie George, John Radford and Ray Kennedy – the team began to show promise. In 1968 and 1969, Arsenal reached two successive League Cup Finals against Leeds United and Swindon Town respectively. Although they lost both matches, the following season the club won its first European trophy – Arsenal's first trophy in 17

ABOVE Bertie Mee standing in front of a bust of former manager, Herbert Chapman in the marbled entrance to Highbury

years – where they beat Anderlecht to claim the Inter-Cities' Fairs Cup.

This victory was only a warm-up and Arsenal went on to win the League and FA Cup Double in 1971, after which he was named Manager of the Year. During 1970-71 Arsenal were unbeaten at home in the League season – a rare occurrence for any club – and they beat their rivals Tottenham Hotspur at White Hart Lane on the last day of the season to claim the League title. Five days later, the Gunners beat Liverpool 2-1 at Wembley in extra time with a winning goal from Charlie George. However, success was not to last and they lost the 1972 Cup Final against Leeds United.

Mee announced his resignation in 1976, but went on to join Watford as general manager, working with Graham Taylor in 1978. As chief scout he was credited with discovering John Barnes. He retired in 1986 but remained a director of the Hornets until 1991. Bertie Mee was made an OBE in 1984 for services to football and died on 22 October 2001.

Mercer

AFTER PLAYING FOR HIS LOCAL club, Ellesmere Port, as winger, Joe Mercer (born on 9 August 1914) joined Everton in September 1932, aged 18. He was a powerful tackler, good at anticipating moves from the opposition, so quickly established himself as a regular first-team midfielder.

He made 186 appearances for Everton, scoring two goals and winning a League Championship medal as well as gaining five caps for England. Due to Second World War, Mercer lost out on seven seasons of football, although he did play 26 wartime internationals, many of them as captain.

A severe cartilage injury went unrecognised and Mercer had to pay for surgery himself. Understandably upset, Mercer moved to Highbury in 1946 for £9,000. At Arsenal, he quickly became captain and won an FA Cup winner's medal in 1950 along with League Championship medals in 1947-48 and 1952-53.

During the 1953-54 season, Mercer was forced to retire after breaking his leg in two places in a match against

RIGHT Joe Mercer, the Arsenal captain, in action against Spurs in 1950

BELOW Joe Mercer enters the pitch carrying the ball

Liverpool. He made 275 appearances for Arsenal and was voted Football Writers' Association Footballer of the Year in 1950.

Mercer went on to become manager of Sheffield United, where lack of experience resulted in relegation, before taking up the manager's job at Aston Villa. He went on to success as a manager at Manchester City between 1965-72 where the club won the First Division (1968), FA Cup (1969), League Cup (1970) and the European Cup Winners' Cup (1970). Mercer was awarded the OBE in 1976 and died on his 76th birthday in 1990.

Merson

MUCH-COVETED TEENAGER PAUL Merson (born 20 March 1968) chose Arsenal over Chelsea, Queens Park Rangers and Watford, turning apprentice in 1984. Apart from seven games on loan to West London neighbours Brentford in 1986-87, he would remain an Arsenal man for the next 13 years despite well-publicised drink, drugs and gambling problems.

With club success came international recognition. Paul won his first cap as substitute against Germany in 1991, and ended up earning 20 more, scoring his first goal for England against Czechoslovakia in a 1992 draw.

November 1996 would see Merson celebrate the tenth anniversary of his first-team debut in an Arsenal shirt, against Manchester City. Entering the fray as substitute for then-Gunner Niall Quinn, he emulated his first full game against Wimbledon by scoring the winning goal.

Paul Merson joined Middlesbrough, recently relegated from the Premiership, in a £4,500,000 deal in the summer of 1997. He made 45 League appearances

in 1997-98, helping the club towards an immediate return to the Premiership and a place in the Coca-Cola Cup Final. Moving to Aston Villa in 1998, he battled his personal problems before helping Portsmouth to the top flight. Dropping to lower-league Walsall as a player in 2003 gave him his first opportunity in management the following year. Inevitably he found it hard to combine on and off-field roles and with the Saddlers struggling he was sacked in 2006. A brief playing return with non-League Tamworth followed.

Though 'Merse' will be remembered for battling his personal problems in public, a career of over 550 League appearances over two decades is no mean achievement.

ABOVE Merson tangles with ex-teammate Michael Thomas during the Coca-Cola Cup in 1996

BELOW Merson in action against Wimbledon in 1997

Neill

WILLIAM JOHN TERENCE Neill (born in Belfast on 8 May 1942) was a solid, unspectacular centre-half who captained both Arsenal and Northern Ireland. He would go on to manage both his country (from 1971 to 1975) and the club after a brief spell at the helm of north London rivals Spurs. His Arsenal playing career spanned the 1960s, playing over 250 times and winning 59 Northern Ireland caps.

In 1970 he left Highbury for Hull City, where he was player-manager, and in 1974 he returned to London for two seasons at White Hart Lane. These were notably unsuccessful, so it was a surprise when he returned to N5 as Bertie Mee's replacement.

Three consecutive Cup Finals between 1978 and 1980 brought just the one win, against Manchester United in 1979, while the Final of the Cup Winners' Cup was reached: the result was defeat to Valencia on penalties. Arsenal's League standing declined

in consecutive years from third in 1981 to fifth, then tenth, and the board felt they had to stop the rot.

Terry Neill gave way to Don Howe in 1983 and decided to pursue a career away from football as owner of a chain of sports bars in and around London.

Nicholas

GLASWEGIAN 'CHAMPAGNE' Charlie Nicholas (born 30 December 1961) began his career with Scottish giants Celtic, making his senior bow in 1980. Successive Championships in 1982 and 1983 were secured thanks to his goalscoring prowess – 50 goals coming in the latter season – and set him up for the title of Player of the Year from both the Scottish football writers and his playing peers.

A move south came in 1983, but five years at Highbury could not match his amazing success in Scotland and he returned north of the border with only a League Cup medal (won by his two goals in 1987) to show for his efforts. Aberdeen paid £400,000 for him, exactly half his earlier price tag, as new Arsenal manager George Graham sought to fashion his own hardworking side.

A return to Celtic and a final season with Second Division Clyde in 1996 seemed to spell the end of his ambitions, but the personable Scot with the

diamond earring and flashing smile has since carved a place for himself among the pundits of Sky Sports where he talks a good game to this day. Unfortunately his medals cabinet and international caps (a total of 20, five goals) do not reflect his talent, though he was something of a Highbury fan favourite. His two goals against Spurs in the first season are fondly remembered, as are his League Cup brace, though a total of 50 in 184 appearances is not spectacular.

Norris

SIR HENRY NORRIS'S CHAIRMAN-ship of Arsenal was as influential as it was controversial. Norris became Mayor of Fulham and Conservative MP for Fulham East. As a director and then chairman of Fulham FC, he oversaw their rise from the Southern League to the Football League. But by 1910, Norris and his business associates had acquired the assets of the ailing Woolwich Arsenal.

Norris's intention was to merge the two clubs or, as a plan B, to base both clubs at Craven Cottage. Not only was the 'superclub' notion dismissed by the Football League but Norris was told he could not control two clubs. So he resigned from Fulham. He then used his political nous to ensure that the Woolwich club overrode local objections to a move to Highbury in 1913, and very soon dropped 'Woolwich' from the club's name.

Norris used his influence to get Arsenal promoted to the newly structured First Division in 1919, the Gunners controversially getting the final nod at the expense of – guess who? – Tottenham Hotspur! But his dodgy dealings finally caught up with him; an alleged 'bung' to Charles Buchan was made public in 1927, then it was suggested that he made personal use of the club's expense accounts. The FA banned him from football in 1929.

By then, though, Norris had made a key appointment; after sacking manager Leslie Knighton, the chairman took on Herbert Chapman. Arsenal FC was on a roll.

BELOW Sir Henry Norris with the 1920-21 Arsenal Squad

O'Leary

BORN IN LONDON OF IRISH parentage on 2 May 1958, David O'Leary was brought up in Dublin but returned to the British capital in 1973 as an Arsenal apprentice. Breaking into the first team at just 17, he displayed an assured touch at centre-back, marking him out as a future stalwart for club and country. Mysteriously he was only Arsenal captain for less than two seasons in the 1980s.

Having started so young he was assured of appearance records given his relative freedom from injuries and when he left for Leeds on a free transfer in 1993 his games in all competitions at all levels ran to four figures, 722 being first team. His international career with Eire brought him 68 caps and the distinction of hitting the sudden-death penalty that beat Romania at the 1990 World Cup finals.

He graduated to assistant manager at Elland Road under former Arsenal favourite George Graham, succeeding him in 1998. But his four-year reign ended controversially with Leeds in financial freefall and a lengthy court

case involving Lee Bowyer, after which O'Leary published an ill-advised book. He went on to take charge of Aston Villa in 2003, but it seemed his managerial career was unlikely to rival his playing record.

Parlour

ROMFORD-BORN RAY PARLOUR (7 March 1973) rarely hit the headlines during his time at Highbury but was an effective midfield presence who kept the team ticking. He made his debut against Liverpool in January 1992 and by the following season had worked his way into first-team contention.

He excelled in the Wembley Cup and League Cup Finals against Sheffield Wednesday, stifling their playmaker Chris Waddle. He also made the team for the two European Finals of succeeding seasons, proving every bit as successful against international opposition and impressing against Real Zaragoza in the second.

Though in and out of the reckoning under Bruce Rioch, who initially saw Ray as a squad player, Parlour was a regular starter under Arsène Wenger and played a major role in securing the 1997-98 Double. The following season he was voted Supporters' Player of the Year.

The 2001-02 Double was another triumph, topped by a goal in the FA Cup Final, but three red cards in a season blemished Parlour's hitherto commendable disciplinary record. As he had gained 10 England caps, he was disappointed not to be taken to Japan for the 2002 World Cup.

Injuries blighted his next two seasons and with increasing competition for midfield places Ray moved to the Riverside in the summer of 2004 to pursue his career with Middlesbrough. Forty-one games in his first season vindicated his decision. Arsenal fans would remember him fondly.

Pires

ROBERT PIRES (BORN 29 OCTOBER 1973) joined Arsenal in the summer of 2000. The established French international was a snip at £5 million, after a traumatic last season with Olympique Marseille had seen his value drop. Primarily a left-winger, Pires can play all across the midfield. This versatility has seen him become a favourite of manager Arsène Wenger.

Known more so for his goalscoring ability than his defensive attributes, Pires began his career at FC Metz in 1993, scoring an impressive 43 times in 171 appearances. Rewarded with a £5 million transfer to Marseille, Pires missed out on the Ligue 1 title by a point in only his first season at the club. His second season was less memorable with problems on and off the pitch, which saw him depart for the Premiership with the Gunners. Despite this, he still managed to clock up 13 goals in 88 appearances.

In 2002 World Cup winner Pires was named Football Writers' Player of the Year, only the fifth Arsenal player in their history to receive the accolade.

ABOVE Robert Pires battles for the ball with Robbie Keane of Spurs in 2006

Despite a reputation for being somewhat flamboyant (he was accused of diving to gain a penalty against Portsmouth at Highbury in the 2003-04 season), his strengths have shone through, proved by the fact he was in demand with clubs at the top level when released by Arsenal in 2006.

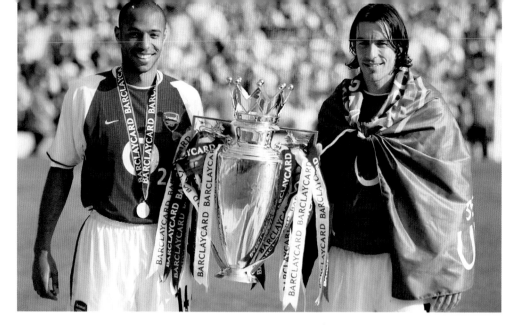

Premiership

ARSENAL'S START TO THE PREMIership was mediocre to say the least. Tenth position in the inaugural season of 1992-93 was disappointing and stemmed from their inability to score: they netted only 40 goals in their 42 League games.

The same problem dogged them the following season when they scored 53 times in 42 games, drawing 17 times on their way to fourth (21 points behind Champions Manchester United). The divide between Arsenal and Premiership winners Blackburn Rovers grew even wider in 1994-95 with the Gunners finishing a massive 38 points off the pace in 12th position.

Fifth and third in the following two seasons preceded an eight-year spell from 1997-98 to 2004-05 when they never finished outside the top two.

The 1997-98 campaign was notable for Ian Wright breaking Cliff Bastin's 81-year-old club scoring record when he netted his 179th goal for Arsenal at Bolton in

September 1997 (Thierry Henry has since eclipsed Wright's achievement). It was also the season when Arsenal claimed their second Double.

As the season drew to a close, Arsenal entered May knowing that they needed just one victory in their final three matches to claim their first Premiership title. Relegation-threatened Everton were the visitors to Highbury on 3 May, a Bilic own goal and strikes from Marc Overmars (2) and Tony Adams giving the Gunners a 4-0 win. The fact that they lost their last two games away to Liverpool and Aston Villa enabled Manchester United to close the gap to one point, making the finish seem tighter than it actually was.

One point again separated the two teams the following season but it was United who reclaimed the title. Arsenal needed to win against Villa on the last day of the season and hope that Spurs could either draw or win at Old Trafford. Arsenal did as much as they could, registering a 1-0 victory, but goals from David Beckham and former Gunner Andy Cole wrecked their celebrations.

ABOVE Celebrations at Highbury in May 2002 after beating Everton 4-3 to win the Premiership

Quinn

BORN ON 6 OCTOBER 1966, Dubliner 'Quinny' was one of a long line of gifted Irishmen to wear an Arsenal shirt. He served the Republic with equal distinction, and with 21 goals in 91 appearances was their all-time leading scorer until his total was surpassed by Robbie Keane.

Scoring on his Arsenal debut in 1985, two years after arriving from Manortown United, the tall striker was a fixture in the 1986-87 team that won the League Cup in manager George Graham's first season but only played 93 matches during his time at Highbury, scoring 20 goals. He was, like Ray Kennedy before him, surprisingly skilful for such a big man (6 foot 5 inches).

He signed for Manchester City in 1990 for a bargain £800,000 fee on being displaced by Alan Smith and moved on to Sunderland six years later for £1.3 million after over 200 appearances in light blue. He became a legend on Wearside where his 'little and large' combination with Kevin Phillips shot them to the promised land of the Premiership.

Quinn retired from professional football, age 37, in 2002, the year his testimonial match raised a reported £1 million for children's charities. He has since become a television and newspaper pundit and in 2006 fronted a takeover bid for Sunderland. Had Arsenal known how his career would develop they would surely never have let him go.

Radford

THE STRIKE PARTNERSHIP OF JOHN Radford and Ray Kennedy that brought the Double to north London was forged from two northerners. Radford hailed from Pontefract, Yorkshire, where he was born on 22 February 1947, and played the experienced campaigner to Kennedy's gifted youth.

With a strike record in League games of better than one in four, Radford's value to the side lay not only in goals. Of equal importance was his supreme ability to play target man, often with little direct support, holding up the ball until the midfield could add strength in numbers. Two England caps, against Romania and Switzerland in 1969 and 1972, were scant reward for his efforts.

Radford's placid temperament and resistance to injury are reflected in an impressive appearance record, missing just one game in the Double season. He

ABOVE Radford leaps over Leicester City goalkeeper Gordon Banks during a First Division match at Highbury in 1965

was voted Arsenal's Player of the Year twice, in 1968 and 1973.

The arrival of young Irishman Frank Stapleton spelled the end of the road for Radford, who spent a miserable, scoreless period at West Ham (ironically, the team he'd made his League debut against back in 1964) after an £80,000 transfer in 1976 before rediscovering his goal touch in a single season at Ewood Park in 1978. The latter year saw his service noted by a testimonial against Spurs, recognition of his tireless contribution to Arsenal's glory years.

John Radford later combined a licensee's career in Essex with non-League management, notably with Bishops Stortford.

Reyes

EXCITING STRIKER JOSE Antonio Reyes' transfer to Arsenal from Spanish side Seville raised a few eyebrows at the turn of 2004, many quoting his price tag – a club record fee of £17.5million – as too high for a player his age. But a brace of goals against Chelsea to knock them out of the 2005 FA Cup left his critics silenced and the Highbury faithful cheering his name.

Whether partnering Thierry Henry up front, or being utilised as a left-winger, Reyes has proved his worth to the Gunners with goals and assists. Despite reports of homesickness in 2005, the Spaniard (born 1 September 1983) squashed speculation by signing a new six-year deal later in the year.

Being a regular in the Spanish national side has given Reyes the experience in big games. However, he holds the dubious title of being only the second player ever to be sent off in an FA Cup Final when he received a second yellow card in 2005 against Manchester United. Reyes returned to Spain on loan in 2006, Brazilian forward Julio Baptista moving to the Emirates from Real Madrid in a temporary player exchange.

RIGHT Jose Antonio Reyes battles for the ball during the Champions League Quarter-Final Second Leg match against Juventus at the Delle Alpi Stadium, 2006

BELOW Reyes vies with West Bromwich's Ronnie Wallwork in April 2006

Rice

'MR RELIABILITY' PAT RICE, WHO returned to Arsenal's staff as youth coach in 1984 and has been assistant manager since 1996, was always bound for Highbury from the very outset. He even went to school in the shadow of the ground, despite a birthplace of Belfast (where he made his appearance on 17 March 1949) qualifying him to captain his country.

Signing apprentice forms at Christmas 1964, Patrick James Rice made his League bow three Yuletides later against Burnley. There then followed 13 glorious years before his £8,000 transfer to Watford in 1980 – years that took in the Double, another FA Cup win (plus three runners-up medals) and 49 Northern Ireland cups.

He learned the captain's art from Frank McLintock, and would in time take over from him as Highbury skipper. But as Double manager Bertie Mee explains Rice was all raw talent and by no means the finished article when he first arrived.

'We signed him because he lived 200 yards from the ground and we were short of full-backs,' says Mee of someone he dubbed a 'self-made man and a dedicated professional. If you told him to improve any aspect of his play, then he would be in for extra work.'

The Double season was Pat's first full campaign, having benefited from Mee's decision to move stalwart Peter Storey to wing-half. Rice responded, missing only the second game of the season and

BELOW Pictured in 1971, Pat Rice is waiting for a corner to be taken

proving a solid performer. It's a tribute to the man that no fewer than four players – Devine, Hollins, Robson and Hill – disputed the position before Viv Anderson's arrival on the scene in 1984.

If Pat missed out on completing his half-century of international caps (he already had two at Under-23 level), he enjoyed an Indian summer at Watford where he made over 100 appearances, scoring one goal. As Arsenal's youth coach he confirmed his ability by securing the FA Youth Cup twice, in 1988 and 1994. In September 1996, after Stewart Houston's departure, he was caretaker manager for four first-team games, three won. He now assists Arsène Wenger with all the composure and reliability for which he was known as a player.

Rice has, with Bob Wilson, been involved in all three Arsenal Doubles, as player and, latterly, coach.

BELOW Prince Charles presenting captain Pat Rice with the 1979 FA Cup after his team beat Manchester United 3-2

Rix

A CULTURED MIDFIELDER who deserved his 17 England caps, Graham Rix emerged in the post-Double period to stamp his authority on the Gunners' midfield, initially with and later succeeding the influential Liam Brady.

Born 23 October 1957 in Doncaster, he joined Arsenal as an apprentice in 1974 but had to wait until the end of the 1976-77 season to make his League debut. He crossed for Alan Sunderland's FA Cup Final winner in 1979, but the following year missed a penalty in the shootout for the Cup Winners' Cup. He made his England debut under Ron Greenwood against Norway in 1981 and remained on the international scene for three further years. He was appointed captain in 1983 but a recurring Achilles tendon injury sustained in November that year saw him out of action for long periods thereafter. As younger hopefuls like Paul Davis and David Rocastle pushed for opportunities his appearances in an Arsenal shirt became fewer and further between.

Granted a free transfer in the summer of 1988, Rix joined forces with former England team-mate Glenn Hoddle at Premiership Chelsea. He then embarked on a managerial career which included spells at Portsmouth, Oxford and Hearts.

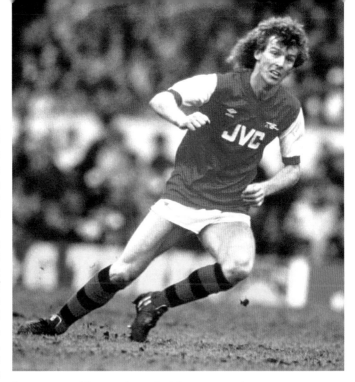

ABOVE Graham Rix in action for the Gunners

Rocastle

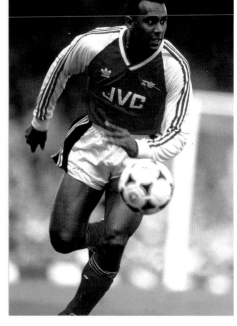

DAVID ROCASTLE WAS AN elegant but determined attacking midfielder, much loved by the Highbury faithful, who won two League Championship medals with Arsenal. Born in Lewisham on 2 May 1967, he came through Arsenal's junior ranks to make his debut in a goalless draw against Newcastle United in September 1985. He picked up his first major winner's medal in 1987 when Arsenal beat Liverpool in the League (Milk) Cup Final at Wembley. His first Championship medal came in 1989, by which time he was very much a fixture in the side, playing in all 38 games as the Gunners pulled off a thrilling 2-0 win at Anfield to pip Liverpool.

Arsenal won the title again in 1991, but this time 'Rocky' played in only 18 matches because of a knee injury. By the time he was surprisingly sold to Leeds for £2 million in 1992, he had also picked up 14 England caps. However, further injury and strong competition

RIGHT Rocastle runs with the ball, 1989

BELOW Portrait of David Rocastle

for places resulted in a mere 25 appearances before he was transferred to Manchester City.

It was the same script at Maine Road, though, and also at Chelsea. Loan spells at Norwich City and Hull City followed before a two-year stint for Malaysian side Sabah. He retired in 2000. A year later the football world was shocked when he died from non-Hodgkin's lymphoma. Poignantly, Rocky's nine-year-old son, Ryan, led the Arsenal team out in the FA Cup Final later that year.

Royal Arsenal

DIAL SQUARE FC TRANSFORMED into Royal Arsenal on Christmas Day 1886 when the players met in the Royal Oak, next to Woolwich Arsenal station.

Included in this group were two former Nottingham Forest players, Morris Bates and Fred Beardsley. The latter wrote to his old club seeking help as the fledgling club could not afford to buy shirts for every player and they responded with a full set of red jerseys and a ball.

Nicknamed the Reds, Royal Arsenal's inaugural fixture took place on Plumstead Common on 8 January 1887 when neighbours Erith were convincingly beaten 6-0. Of their ten friendly games that season, they lost just two: away to Millwall Rovers and the 2nd Rifle Brigade.

Playing their home ties at first Plumstead Common, then the Sportsman Ground and finally the Manor Ground, Royal Arsenal enjoyed success in local cup competitions. Although winning the London Charity Cup and the Kent Senior Cup in 1889-90 and the London Cup (they beat St Bart's Hospital 6-0 in the Final) the following season meant higher-calibre players wanted to turn out for the club.

This also attracted the unwanted attention of professional teams, so it was proposed at the 1891 AGM that the club turn professional themselves and the name be changed to Woolwich Arsenal.

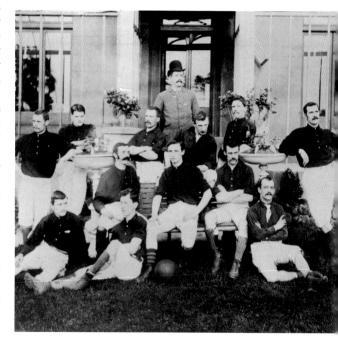

BELOW The Royal Arsenal football squad. Previously known as Dial Square and then Woolwich Arsenal, the team became known simply as Arsenal in 1914

Sansom

BORN IN CAMBERWELL on 26 September 1958, left-back Kenny Sansom started his professional career with Crystal Palace where he was a member of Terry Venables' famed 'Team of the 1980s' that won promotion to the top flight and provided the future Spurs manager with his first taste of non-playing success.

During his time at Selhurst Park, Sansom registered 172 League appearances (three goals) before Terry Neill dangled striker Clive Allen as bait to win his signature in a sensational £1.25 million swap in 1980. Record books show that he was the first 'million-pound full-back', though the Gunners' reserve keeper Paul Barron was also part of a confusing equation.

By this time, the player – a former England Youth captain – had already claimed the first of 86 full caps for his country. He was clearly the answer to the problem left-back position. He also captained Arsenal to consecutive League Cup Finals, winning in 1987 and picking up a losers' medal a year later. (By this time Tony Adams had succeeded him as captain.)

'Norman', as Sansom was known by his team-mates due to a deadly accurate impression of funny man Norman Wisdom, belied his diminutive stature to prove a polished performer whose on-field standards never slipped. Unfortunately Arsenal underachieved during most of his spell with the club, leaving him short in the medals tally.

His England career began against Wales in the 1979 Home Internationals, ending in 1988 with his final cap against the USSR. Bobby Robson's team had performed poorly in the European Championships, and in the run-up to the 1990 World Cup Nottingham Forest's Stuart Pearce would be preferred. But Pearce could not eclipse Sansom, the seventh most capped England player, as England's most capped full-back, ending his career with 78. (Gary Neville looks set to beat both of these records.)

A disagreement with manager George Graham in the summer of 1988 saw Kenny replaced as first choice by ex-Wimbledon man Nigel Winterburn, who would prove equally as reliable. He had played 394 times for the Gunners, scoring six goals. Jim Smith signed Sansom for Newcastle, but he returned to QPR to play under former Gunner Don Howe (1989-91). Spells followed at Coventry (1991-93), Everton and Watford (1994).

Having weathered business and gambling problems in his personal life, the likeable Sansom is now a regular pundit on TV and LBC radio.

BELOW Kenny Sansom in action

Seaman

SOLID AND RELIABLE RATHER THAN flamboyant, Yorkshire-born David 'Safe Hands' Seaman (born 19 September 1963) took the steady and unspectacular route to the top. His period with Arsenal coincided with the status of England Number 1 keeper.

His journey started at Leeds, where Seaman was an apprentice but failed to make a senior appearance. A £4,000 move to London Road, Peterborough in 1982, brought him first-team football, and he made the most of the chance: when he moved to Birmingham City a little over two seasons later his value had shot up to six figures.

By the time he received his first England cap against Saudi Arabia in November 1988 David was at Queens Park Rangers, whom he'd joined two years earlier for £225,000. But with

squad he returned for England's World Cup 2002 campaign. England's man of the match in the 1-1 opener with Sweden, he was caught off his line for Brazil's second goal – Ronaldinho's mis-hit free-kick – as England lost 2-1. He would give up his position to David James, but clocked up an impressive 75 caps.

On the club front, Seaman found success from the start, playing in the 1991 title-winning team and in both of the 1993 Cup Finals. He also starred in the two European Cup Winners' Cup campaigns – one successful, the other less so – that followed. And though he was blamed for letting in Nayim's last-minute winner in 1995, it was only his inspired performance in a penalty shootout in Genoa that took the Gunners to the Final in the first place.

Moving to Manchester City in June 2003 after 13 successful years at Highbury, he took with him two FA Premier League winner's medals and four FA Cup winner's medals. Sadly his spell under Kevin Keegan would end prematurely through injury in 2004, but he had the consolation of being voted into the Premier League Team of the Decade in the 10 Seasons Awards poll.

Arsenal looking for a younger successor to John Lukic – who, ironically would return to Leeds, David's first club – he made the lucrative trip across the capital to Highbury the following year for £1.3 million.

Together with club colleague centre-back Tony Adams, he gave the England defence their foundation for many years. He had an excellent Euro 2000 in Holland and Belgium, and though Sven Goran Eriksson left Seaman out of his first

BELOW Seaman celebrates during the match against his first club, Leeds United, September 2002

Simpson

SOLID AND DEPENDABLE, EAST Anglian central defender Simpson was one of the cornerstones on which Arsenal's Double triumph of 1970-71 was built.

After playing junior football for Gorleston Town, Norfolk-born Simpson (born 13 January 1945) went for trials at Crystal Palace but eventually ended up on the other side of London – and, indeed, made his League debut in 1964 against another capital outfit, Chelsea. Not quite a six-footer, he played a Bobby Moore-style role, and indeed missed out on England recognition due to the presence of Moore and Norman Hunter: Simpson was a member of Alf Ramsey's 1970 World Cup party of 40, but failed to make the 22 who travelled.

He had, however, been made Arsenal Player of the year in 1969, and would go on to play a major part in honours to come. Bertie Mee pinpointed his failing as a lack of aggression. 'It was a pity he had to be kicked up the backside all the time.' Nevertheless, Mee was full of admiration for a player he believed was the most composed man in the Double-winning back four who had 'great talent… he should have had 50 caps for England…'

Nearing the veteran stage in the mid 1970s, Simpson was squeezed out of contention by the developing David O'Leary and the expensively-signed Willie Young and left Highbury in 1978. He joined the exodus to the North American Soccer League but, after a spell with the New England Teamen, returned to play for non-League Hendon.

BELOW Few forwards ruffled Gunners defender Peter Simpson

Stapleton

A BIG, BUSTLING TARGET MAN OF the old school but with a surprisingly subtle touch, Dublin-born Frank Stapleton (born 10 July 1956) was rejected by Manchester United before Arsenal signed him up. His years as a first-teamer at Highbury from 1973 to 1981 saw him score 75 goals in 225 League appearances, and he scored in the memorable 3-2 FA Cup win over the Red Devils in 1979 to prove they had been wrong.

His initial strike partnership was with Malcolm Macdonald, but it was in harness with Alan Sunderland that he finished Arsenal's top scorer in three consecutive season from 1978-80. A regular choice for the Republic of Ireland, Stapleton won 71 caps over 13 years, scoring 20 goals, and took as much pleasure in making goals as claiming them.

Ironically, his next port of call after Highbury was Old Trafford, and he came within two League games of his Arsenal total in a different red shirt in a spell that stretched from 1981 to 1987. (His goal in 1983 made him the first player to score for two clubs in two Wembley FA Cup Finals.) A string of further clubs, most notably Blackburn Rovers and (as player-manager) Bradford City, saw him end his career in the States. He occasionally pops up as a TV pundit, having been a legend with two of England's leading clubs.

ABOVE Whole-hearted striker Frank Stapleton scored 75 League goals for Arsenal

Storey

PETER STOREY ADDED THE steel to the 1971 Double side, and was so admired for his hard but fair play that he gained 19 full caps for his country between 1971 and 1973.

Born Peter Edwin Storey in Farnham, Surrey on 7 September 1945, he was introduced by Billy Wright in 1965 as full-back, where he proved a suitable replacement for the veteran Don Howe.

He stayed in the side in that role until new manager Bertie Mee switched him to midfield at the start of the Double season; he responded by playing all but two League games in that campaign. Mee described the man he inherited as 'an honest, hard professional – not a dirty player but a whole-hearted one. He gave everything he had.' He also had a steady nerve, which made him a prolific scorer from the penalty spot over the years.

Storey retained a regular first-team place until 1975, despite strong competition from Eddie Kelly. A deadline-day 1977 move to Fulham for £11,000 didn't bring the Cottagers their money's worth. He retired from football that November due to injury, later running a pub in Islington and a market stall in London's West End.

RIGHT The backbone of the 1975 Arsenal defence was supported by Peter Storey

BELOW Peter Storey holds off Eddie Gray of Leeds United

Thomas

MICHAEL THOMAS SIGNED AS A schoolboy for Arsenal in 1982 before turning professional in 1984. Born on 24 August 1967, his first-team career began with a debut in the first leg of the League Cup semi-final against Tottenham Hotspur on 8 February 1987.

Thomas soon became a regular in the first team, playing 37 times, mainly at right-back in 1987-88 but, with the arrival of Lee Dixon was moved forward into midfield the following season. He also won his first cap for England in a friendly against Saudi Arabia.

His greatest moment came with the goal he scored for Arsenal against Liverpool in the final minute of the final First Division match on 26 May 1989. Liverpool had already won the FA Cup and were in with a chance of winning a second Double.

Thomas's surge from midfield and a low shot past Bruce Grobbelaar during injury time meant that Arsenal secured the two goals they needed and the League title – their first in 18 years.

Thomas stayed another two seasons at Arsenal, winning a second League title in 1991, playing a total of 206 matches and scoring 30 goals before falling out with manager George Graham. He was sold to Liverpool, but injuries blighted his career and – after stints with Middlesbrough, Benfica and Wimbledon – he retired in 2001.

BELOW Michael Thomas (left) and Martin Hayes after the Division One match against Liverpool at Anfield in 1989 that clinched the League title

UEFA Cup

ARSENAL'S FIRST VENTURE INTO the Inter-Cities Fairs Cup in 1963-64 saw them paired with Staevnet. A 7-1 first-leg win in Denmark with Strong and Baker netting a hat-trick each preceded a 4-2 aggregate exit at the hands of Standard Liege in the second round.

By the time they next qualified in 1969-70, the tournament was called the European Fairs Cup. Victories in the opening rounds over Glentoran (3-1 aggregate), Sporting Club de Portugal (3-0), Rouen (1-0) and Dinamo Bacau (9-1) set up a Semi-Final clash with Ajax. Winning the home leg 3-0 meant that a 1-0 reverse in Amsterdam did not halt their progress in the competition. Having lost the first leg of the Final 3-1 against Anderlecht, a remarkable second leg saw the Gunners triumph 4-3 on aggregate to claim their first European trophy.

The defence of their title the following season came to an end against FC Koln in the Fourth Round with Arsenal drawing 2-2 on aggregate but being eliminated on the away goals rule.

They failed to progress through the early stages of their next three campaigns – losing to Red Star Belgrade (1978-79, Third Round), KFC Winterslag (1980-81, Second Round, again on away goals) and Spartak Moscow (1982-83, First Round) – before the post-Heysel ban on British clubs competing in Europe.

Although this ban was lifted at the start of the 1990s, Arsenal's attention was centred on the Cup Winners' Cup so it was 1996-97 before they again qualified for the UEFA Cup. It was a short-lived campaign, however, with Borussia Moenchengladbach ending their interest in the First Round. The Gunners were again eliminated on away goals in the First Round tie with PAOK Saloniki the following season.

New rules were introduced by UEFA and, having been knocked out of the first phase of the 1999-2000 Champions League, Arsenal were automatically entered into the Third Round of that season's UEFA Cup.

Nantes and Deportivo La Coruna were both brushed aside with an identical 6-3 aggregate score while Werder Bremen went down 6-2 over both legs. Home (1-0) and away (2-1) victories over Lens set up a Final meeting with Turks Galatasaray in Copenhagen, scene of the 1994 Cup Winners' Cup triumph.

Unfortunately, the Gunners lost 4-1 on penalties after extra time had failed to bring a goal from either side.

Unbeaten Run

WHEN PRESTON NORTH END WON the inaugural First Division campaign in 1888-89, they finished the season undefeated (indeed, they dropped just four points from their 22 games). When Arsenal managed to complete the 2003-04 season unbeaten, they became only the second team ever to achieve this feat and eclipsed the 42-match record of top-flight unbeaten games set by Brian Clough's Nottingham Forest in their 1977-78 heyday.

The Gunners' 49-game unbeaten

BELOW Thierry Henry celebrates with teammates after scoring Arsenal's second goal against Wolverhampton during a Premier League match at Highbury in 2003

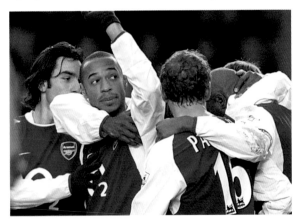

run began with the last two matches of 2002-03 against Southampton (6-1) and Sunderland (4-0) before they kicked off the new season on 16 August with a 2-1 at home to Everton, Henry and Pires scoring the home side's goals. Talismanic French striker Henry would contribute 30 of his team's 73 League goals that campaign while his compatriot netted an impressive 14 from midfield.

Some of the highlights of the season were doubles over Middlesbrough (4-0 away, 4-1 home), Leeds United (4-1 away, 5-0 home) and a particularly enjoyable 4-2 home victory over Liverpool in April. Of the visitors to fortress Highbury, only Portsmouth, Fulham, Manchester United and Birmingham City managed to steal any points.

Arsenal clinched the Premiership title with a 2-2 draw at White Hart Lane (echoes of the 1970-71 Double!) on 25 April and, with just four games to go, the dream was becoming a reality. Draws against Birmingham and Portsmouth preceded a single-goal victory over Fulham at Craven Cottage so the finale was set for the visit of already-relegated Leicester City.

Although former Highbury favourite Paul Dickov threatened to ruin the day with a first-half strike, goals from Henry and Vieira sent north London wild. Arsenal had finished the season without losing a single game; second-placed Chelsea lost seven games during the 2003-04 season and finished 11 points behind.

The 2004-05 campaign carried on where the previous one had finished, with Arsenal registering eight wins in their opening nine games. With the magic 50 in their sights, the Gunners went to Old Trafford on 24 October 2004 but goals from Ruud van Nistelrooy (a controversial penalty) and Wayne Rooney (in injury time) brought their undefeated run to an end.

No matter how it ended (for the record, the 49-game run lasted 542 days and featured 36 wins, 13 draws, 108 goals for and 34 against), Arsenal are rightly proud of their achievement which, in today's highly competitive game, might last for more than a century.

ABOVE Captain Patrick Vieira holds up a specially commissioned trophy for not losing a game in the Premiership in 2003-04

MIDDLE Arsenal celebrate winning the Championship after beating Leicester City, May, 2004

Vieira

WHEN ARSÈNE WENGER ARRIVED at Highbury in 1996 after completing his duties in Japan, he had already ensured one of the cornerstones of his new team was present on his arrival. Patrick Vieira (born 23 June 1976) would prove an inspirational presence in the Gunners midfield for nearly a decade, and his leadership would be crucial in the club's accomplishments under fellow Frenchman Wenger.

Born in the African colony of Senegal but brought up in Paris, Vieira turned pro with Cannes before moving to AC Milan where he was a squad player who failed to gain a regular first-team berth. Spotted by Wenger as an unexploited talent, he was signed for a sum reported variously as £3 and £4 million. He was an integral part of the team that took the Double in 1998, his imposing (6ft 4in) stature belying the fact that he was a box-to-box mid-fielder who linked well with country-man Manu Petit.

Temperament proved a problem, however, and dismissals in the first two games of 2000-01 saw this addressed with the help of Arsène Wenger. Like Roy Keane, with whom he was often compared, he managed to retain his competitive edge without excessive disciplinary layoffs – and like the Irishman would become an inspirational captain. He inherited the armband from Tony Adams in 2002 on the latter's retirement. Internationally Vieira was a regular in the French team, for whom he debuted in 1997 and appeared as sub in the following year's World Cup Final.

Though he'd teetered on the brink of a move to Spain in summer 2004 after France's poor showing at the European

Championships, he finally departed Highbury in 2005 for AC Milan, his last act the winning penalty at the Millennium Stadium to secure the FA Cup in a shootout over rivals Manchester United. His playing record stood at over 400 appearances in the red and white, with three titles and four FA Cups. Vieira was booked when his new team drew his old, however, and had to watch as the Gunners defeated his current employers en route to the 2006 Champions League Final.

While many felt the £14 million received was no replacement for the towering Frenchman, the Gunners' European success combined with Vieira's indifferent showing silenced many critics. At 30-plus, his combative style would henceforth prove harder to maintain – but fans were grateful he gave his best years to Arsenal.

Wembley

WEMBLEY HAS LONG BEEN A HOME from home for Arsenal because apart from hosting Cup Finals, they have also competed there in FA Cup semi-finals and European matches.

As previously documented, Arsenal's first trip to Wembley in 1927 ended in defeat by Cardiff City and resulted in the FA Cup being won by a non-English team for the only time in its history. The Gunners have since been back to contest another 12 FA Cup Finals, winning the famous trophy seven times.

They have also played two FA Cup semi-finals at the stadium, both against neighbours Spurs, when – following the Hillsborough tragedy when 96 Liverpool fans died during the 1989 semi-final – the Football Association decided to stage the tie there so that more fans would be able to see the game in safety. Wembley had not previously been a semi-final

ABOVE Suker and Henry celebrate during the Champions League match against AIK Solna, played at Wembley Stadium, 1999

venue as the FA did not want to detract from the magic of the Final.

A second-half Alan Smith strike was not enough to see off the White Hart Lane outfit in 1991, who – with goals from Paul Gascoigne and Gary Lineker (2) – won their way through to a Final meeting with Nottingham Forest. The clash was repeated two years later and this time Tony Adams managed to get his head to a Paul Merson cross for the only goal of the match.

Wembley also saw Arsenal contest five League Cup Finals (winning three) and six FA Charity Shields (again, winning

three) before the venue was demolished and the showpiece matches moved to Cardiff's Millennium Stadium.

With UEFA stipulating that the Highbury capacity would have to be drastically reduced to comply with their advertising hoarding regulations, Arsenal decided to stage their home UEFA Champions League matches between 1998-99 and 1999-2000 at Wembley Stadium. This allowed more Gunners fans to watch these European ties than Highbury would normally accommodate.

Panathinaikos were the first visitors to Arsenal's new temporary home on 30 September 1998 and goals from Adams and Keown gave the Gunners a 2-1 victory. They were unable to maintain this momentum, however, and could only draw 1-1 with Dynamo Kiev before losing 1-0 to Lens. The following season saw them beat AIK Solna 3-1 before falling to Barcelona (4-2) and Fiorentina (1-0).

Arsenal's sojourn at Wembley had proved none too impressive, winning two, drawing one and losing three of the six games, and the club reverted to playing at Highbury for the 2000-01 campaign.

ABOVE Marc Overmars (left) celebrates his goal during the Charity Shield match against Manchester United, 1998

MIDDLE Arsenal fans waving flags during the FA Cup Final, 1972

Wenger

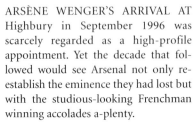

ARSÈNE WENGER'S ARRIVAL AT Highbury in September 1996 was scarcely regarded as a high-profile appointment. Yet the decade that followed would see Arsenal not only re-establish the eminence they had lost but with the studious-looking Frenchman winning accolades a-plenty.

Born in Strasbourg on 22 September 1949, he combined a degree course with playing amateur football. A French title won with Strasbourg in 1979 would be the pinnacle of his achievements on the pitch (though he was not a regular in the team), following which he spent two years gaining a diploma in management and became the club's youth coach.

His first head coaching job at Nancy in 1984, attended by relegation, was followed by a move to Monaco three years later

and the French Championship the year after (the cup was won in 1991). He signed players of the calibre of Jürgen Klinsmann and Glenn Hoddle, but was ignomiously sacked after the side finished ninth. An 18-month spell in Japan with Nagoya Grampus 8 in 1995 was curtailed by Arsenal's call to replace Bruce Rioch.

Success came as early as his second season 1997-98 when the Premiership and FA Cup Double was achieved, a success repeated in 2002 after three consecutive second positions. Fellow Frenchmen like Vieira, Henry and Pires have played a notable part, but his seeming unwillingness to sign British players (Francis Jeffers a notable and unsuccessful exception) has been much remarked upon. Youngsters like Nicolas Anelka and Cesc Fabregas were brought in from Europe as unknowns and, in the former case, sold for a multi-million profit.

2002-03 brought another FA Cup, while the Premiership win in 2004, the third under Wenger, was achieved without a single defeat, the first time this had been achieved since Preston's Invincibles held sway the Football League's first season. The FA Cup was won again in 2005 on penalties over Manchester United. Yet success in Europe proved elusive, so winning through to the European Champions League Final in April 2006 was sweet indeed.

A quiet, studious demeanour has occasionally given way to Gallic passion; spats with Alex Ferguson, Martin Jol and Jose Mourinho have caused raised eyebrows, while Wenger's frequent habit of stating he could not comment on incidents since he could not see them from his touchline position has also been derided. Yet there is little doubt than the majority of clubs in Europe would be delighted to appoint him their manager, and he was mentioned as a candidate to succeed Sven Goran Eriksson as England boss even though he is under contract to Arsenal until 2008.

Wenger's approach to off-field matters such as diet and training has helped revolutionise the club, and he has spearheaded a wave of foreign coaches – Mourinho, Benitez, etc – who have done likewise elsewhere. Awarded the Legion d'Honneur in 2002 and an honorary OBE in 2003, Wenger – known as the Professor to friend and foe alike – has more than made his mark on British football and is now established as Arsenal's most successful manager of all time.

Whittaker

TOM WHITTAKER WAS CHIEF COOK and bottle washer at Arsenal in the first half of the 20th century – player, assistant trainer, trainer, physio and secretary-manager. Born in Army barracks in Aldershot on 21 July 1898, Whittaker joined Arsenal in 1919 first as a centre-forward, but went on to play at left-back and wing-half. He played 70 games in all, scoring twice, but his playing career came to a premature halt in 1925 after injuring his knee on an FA trip to Australia.

Determined to stay in the game, he studied physiotherapy and became assistant trainer (to George Hardy) and then took over from Hardy in 1927, going on to be England trainer. Whittaker completely revised the training and physiotherapy set-up at Highbury, so much so that it became recognised as a centre of excellence, while he also took on the England and FA touring duties.

The Second World War interrupted matters, although Whittaker, typically, led from the front during the hostilities as an RAF squadron leader. When George Allison stood down in 1947, Whittaker, who was awarded the MBE, took over the secretary-manager role and guided Arsenal to the League title in 1948 and 1953 – by the narrowest of goal difference margins – and the FA Cup in 1950.

The strain of running the club became too much, however, and he suffered a fatal heart attack in 1956. The post of secretary-manager was subsequently split in two; Jack Crayston took over as manager, and Bob Wall became secretary.

RIGHT Tom Whittaker discusses tactics with one of his players in 1953

BELOW Tom Whittaker the Arsenal trainer in 1938

Wilson

THOUGH HE BECAME A Scottish international through parentage, Arsenal's Double keeper Robert Primrose 'Bob' Wilson was born on 30 October 1941 and brought up in Chesterfield. Despite successful trials with Manchester United he elected to study at Loughborough University instead of joining them. After a brief period as an amateur with Wolves, he turned his back on a career as a PE teacher when offered a professional contract by the Gunners in 1964. (Technically he made his debut as an amateur, the last to play top-flight football in England.)

After spending time in the reserves, he was first choice when, in 1970 Arsenal won their first major trophy for 17 years, the Fairs (now UEFA) Cup. But Wilson more than played his part in the following year's Double triumph. "I could never repeat those eleven years at Arsenal," he said on retirement, "and there is nothing to match that week in

May. It's a great dream that happens to a lucky few."

It turned out to be his greatest year as, with rules on international qualification changing, he made his international debut in a European Championship game against Portugal that October. Scotland won 2-1 and, though Wilson was to earn only one more cap, he and his father were justly proud of his achievement. He was the first Englishman since 1873 to pull on a

ABOVE Bob Wilson demonstrates his skills during a training session

LEFT Scotland and Arsenal goalkeeper Bob Wilson in 1971

smother the danger. His secret, he said, was consistency. "You have to have a natural ability and be prepared to learn. It's easy to have a great game one day, followed by a bad one. My aim was always to play to a level.'"

Wilson never fully recovered from an injury in the 1972 FA Cup semi-final against Stoke City in 1972, when he twisted and fell awkwardly after gathering a cross. The resulting torn cartilage and damaged ligaments meant he missed the Final against Leeds United, and he retired three years later with a little over three hundred senior appearances to his credit.

Bob Wilson continued his association with Arsenal by becoming goalkeeping coach to both Pat Jennings and David Seaman, as well as carving out a career as a TV anchorman for sports programmes. In this, he was as effective and unfussy as he had been on the pitch. He published his autobiography in 2003.

Scotland shirt, even though he had played for England's youth team.

Wilson was an all-rounder, his one trademark an almost reckless bravery that frequently saw him foiling opponents who broke through the Gunners' rearguard by diving at their feet to

Winterburn

BUT FOR STUART PEARCE, NIGEL Winterburn (born 11 December 1963) would surely have won more than the two England caps he has to his name. At Highbury though, he made the Number 3 shirt his personal property,

Winterburn nearly left the game altogether after the disappointment of being released on a free transfer by his first club Birmingham City in 1983. Luckily he found a happier hunting ground at Plough Lane, Wimbledon, where he made nearly 200 appearances in all competitions and started to catch the eye.

A £400,000 move across London to Highbury found Kenny Sansom the man in possession for club and country. Nigel waited his chance and initially proved his versatility by playing on the right. But time was on his side, and the Arsenal left-back berth brought international recognition and a host of honours. His first Championship came in his first season in the Number 3 shirt, while he also gained winner's medals in the Coca-Cola, FA and Cup Winners' Cups.

ABOVE Winterburn on the ball, 1999

A typically consistent performer, he was one of the George Graham back four that kept a high line and consistently trapped opposing forwards offside. He left Highbury after 12 seasons in the summer for 2000, sensing himself not part of Arsène Wenger's future plans, and enjoyed a great first season with West Ham. But at 35 the writing was on the wall and he retired from football after one more season in the top flight. His career appearances exceeded 850.

Woolwich Arsenal

RIGHT The captains of
Woolwich Arsenal and
Newcastle United shake
hands before the start
of the opening match
of the 1893-94 season

BELOW George
Burdett, the Woolwich
Arsenal goalkeeper,
holding the ball during
a game against
Liverpool

ALTHOUGH THE CLUB CHANGED
its name from Royal Arsenal to
Woolwich Arsenal at the 1891 AGM, the
proposal made at that time to turn professional was not adopted for another
two years.

The club lobbied the Football League
for election in 1893 and, even though
there were no League clubs south of
Birmingham and Burton, the Football
Association realised that in order to go
national, the League must contain
teams in London. Arsenal formed a limited liability company in order to raise
the money required to provide facilities
befitting a League club.

Saturday 2 September 1893 saw the
club's first League outing when the home
side held newly-elected Newcastle United
to a 2-2 draw while 12 December 1896
brought the club's record defeat (an 8-0
reverse away to Loughborough Town).

The arrival of other London clubs in
the League saw Arsenal having to compete for support and the Boer War
(1899-1902) put a huge strain on the

The captains of Woolwich Arsenal and Newcastle United shake hands before the start of the opening match of the 1893-94 season

club's finances as players and supporters were not in the locale to enjoy their
traditional Saturday afternoons, and
in 1908 new manager George Morrell
was forced to sell his best players
to survive.

Bankruptcy was averted by Henry
Norris in 1910 and it was he who mas-
terminded the move to Highbury and
the dropping of the Woolwich part of
the name in 1913.

Wright

ARSENAL'S GREATEST SCORER OF recent times until the arrival of Thierry Henry, Ian Edward Wright (born 3 November 1963) put everything into his performances, just as he does now as a TV pundit, and carved himself a place in Highbury history with his wonder goals.

Wright's professional career took a

long time to take off, but the Woolwich-born player always seemed impatient to make up for lost time. He was still playing for Greenwich Borough in the lower reaches of the non-League game in his early 20s when then Crystal Palace manager Steve Coppell took a chance in bringing him late to the professional ranks. He helped Palace to the FA Cup Final, working well with up-front partner

Mark Bright, and would spend six successful seasons at Selhurst Park.

He won his first four England caps as a Palace player in 1991 and Arsenal pounced to make him a club record purchase. A goal on his debut, a League Cup tie against Leicester, was followed by a hat-trick on his League debut, a 4-0 win at Southampton on 28 September 1991. This won over Gunners fans from the off, and Wright scorched 24 goals in 30 League games as Arsenal finished fourth.

BELOW In 1997, Wright celebrated breaking the Arsenal scoring record set by Cliff Bastin

Wright collected his first winner's medals in 1992-93, two of his ten FA Cup goals that term arriving in the Wembley Finals (Sheffield Wednesday having managed a 1-1 draw in the first game), while he also played in the Coca-Cola Cup Final win against the same opposition.

He missed the 1994 European Cup Winners' Cup win after a personal season of 23 League goals, though he played in the 1995 Final in Paris. His collection of England caps reached 33 in total, thanks to a recall by Glenn Hoddle that saw him help his country to the 1998 World Cup finals. He missed the finals, however, due to injury.

The hero of Highbury notched 185 goals for the Gunners in all competitions but was clearly not going to play a long-term part in Arsène Wenger's plans. He departed in the summer of 1998 for post-Arsenal postscripts with West Ham, Celtic and Burnley. His scoring record for Arsenal was better than a goal every other game, making the £2.5 million which the Gunners forked out for him something of a snip. The family name continues in football, though not (yet) at Arsenal, thanks to Shaun and Bradley Wright-Phillips.

X-Tra Time

WHILE FOOTBALL'S ORGANISING bodies have tried various alternatives to extra time over the years (such as the introduction of the away goals rule and the silver goal), Arsenal do not seem to have fared very well when it has come to playing more than the allotted 90 minutes over the years.

They were disqualified from the Kent County Cup in 1889 for refusing to play extra time with their game against Gravesend tied at 3-3, while Third Division Swindon Town emerged 3-1 victors after extra time in the 1969 League Cup Final.

Arsenal have also lost three European Finals after extra time. Penalties decided their fate in the 1980 Cup Winners' Cup against Valencia and the 2000 UEFA Cup

against Galatasaray while Nayim's 50-yard shot that caught David Seaman off guard denied them the 1995 Cup Winners' Cup and won it for Real Zaragoza.

It has not all been doom and gloom, though. They did claim the 1971 (against Liverpool), 1993 (Sheffield Wednesday) and 2005 (Manchester United) FA Cups after 90 minutes had failed to find a winner. In the match with Sheffield Wednesday, the winning goal arrived in the last minute of extra time, while Arsenal emerged triumphant from a penalty w against United.

ABOVE Arsenal celebrate winning the FA Cup Final at the Millennium Stadium, May, 2005. Manchester United were beaten on penalties after extra time

Youth Team

ABOVE A young Liam Brady parades with other members of the Arsenal youth team carrying the Youth Cup, the League Championship and the FA Cup trophies around Highbury before Arsenal's match against Chelsea in 1971

RIGHT Arsenal celebrate after winning the AXA FA Youth Cup Final, 2001

BELOW A young Tony Adams, 1981

THE CURRENT HEAD OF YOUTH development, Liam Brady, was voted Arsenal's 'Player of the Season' three times before his move to Juventus and has a lot to live up to as Arsenal's youngsters have won the FA Youth Cup on six occasions.

Their first Final appearance ended in a 3-2 loss at the hands of Everton in 1965 but they were back the following season to defeat Sunderland 5-3.

Not to be outdone by their senior counterparts in Arsenal's Double-winning 1970-71 season, the youngsters beat Cardiff City 2-0 in a replay of the 1927 FA Cup Final to win the Youth Cup but it would be another 17 years before they graced the Final again.

Familiar names such as Kevin Campbell and David Hillier were members of the team that thrashed a Doncaster Rovers side that included

Rufus Brevett and Mark Rankine 6-1 in 1988, while Jermaine Pennant starred in Arsenal's 5-1 victory over Coventry City in 2000. A 1994 5-3 victory over Millwall, the second obtained under the tutelage of Pat Rice, was sandwiched by these titles.

Arsenal's most recent success came in 2001 when, in another high-scoring Final, they beat Blackburn Rovers 6-3.

Zero

ARSENAL EQUALLED AC MILAN'S 2004-05 record of seven Champions League clean sheets in a row when they beat Juventus 2-0 in March 2006. Their first six came against Sparta Prague (0-0 away and 3-0 home), Thun (1-0 away), Ajax (0-0 home) and Real Madrid (1-0 away and 0-0 home).

When Arsenal won the 1990-91 First Division title they only conceded 18 goals in 38 games, David Seaman achieving shut-outs in 24 of these including a run of six in consecutive matches from 6 October to 17 November. When the FA and League Cups are added in to the equation, the Gunners kept a staggering 29 clean sheets that season.

Arsenal kept 23 clean sheets in 38 Premiership matches when they finished as runners-up to Manchester United in 1998-99. That season

included a sequence of six clean sheets between 26 December and 6 February, a feat they matched between 21 September and 2 November 1996.

The Gunners' best sequence of Premiership clean sheets, however, came in the Double-winning season of 1997-98 when they managed to shut out the opposition for eight League games between 31 January and 31 March.

ABOVE Lehmann celebrates after saving a penalty in the 2006 Champions League semi-final

Also available

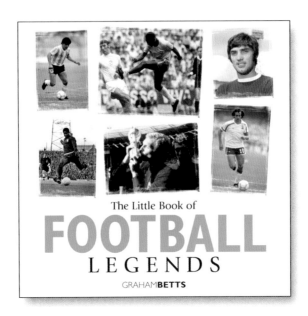

The Little Book of

FOOTBALL

L E G E N D S

GRAHAM**BETTS**

Available from all major book stockists

The pictures in this book were provided courtesy of the following:

GETTY IMAGES
101 Bayham Street, London NW1 0AG

PA PHOTOS
paphotos.com

Book design and artwork by Newleaf Design

Published by Green Umbrella Publishing

Publishers Jules Gammond & Vanessa Gardner

Written by Ian Welch and Michael Heatley with David Lloyd and Julian Heatley